The Doobieous Dictionary
THE A-Z GUIDE TO ALL THINGS CANNABIS

Jason Porter Collinsworth

The Doobieous Dictionary
THE A-Z GUIDE TO ALL THINGS CANNABIS

This book is a work of satire. Any information herein, although often factual, is presented for the sole purpose of entertainment, parody and humor. Any references to historical or recent events, real people, real information, or real locales are used satirically. All other names, characters, places, colloquialisms, phrases and incidents are products of the author's imagination, and any resemblance to actual events, concepts, locales or persons, living or dead, is entirely coincidental.

Edited by Jason Porter Collinsworth and Lara Marie Collinsworth

ISBN-13: 978-1530545445
ISBN-10: 1530545447

For Lara

How to Use This Guide:

Most dictionaries regale a reader with chicken scratch pronunciation and usage guides riddled with semi-nonsensical examples of where to place an accent mark for emphasis.

But, I know exactly where they can shove their marks...

I think y'all are bright enough to figure it the fuck out. So, let's be gettin' on with some higher education.

420 (4:20)- *n.* a term that is applied to all things cannabis, but specifically the times at which one should consume cannabis; *420* has been the subject of much controversy and the center of numerous rumors; if one is to believe all the stories, *420* comes from a penal code for smoking pot invented by The Grateful Dead in reverence to Bob Dylan's *Rainy Day Women #12 and 35* which is the song that the band listened to while getting high at 4:20 every day in high school in Marin, California, to honor *the* Steve DeAngelo since that is the exact time he was supposedly born; in truth, *420* gets its origins from The Waldos, a group of teenagers in San Rafael, California, in the 1970s who would meet up at various locations around school at 4:20 p.m. to get high; from there, it came to mean anything having to do with cannabis and it caught on; supposedly, its current popularity is owed to The Grateful Dead fan nerds called Deadheads who helped spread the term like the sexually transmitted diseases many of them were passing around; also, *420* has become code among workers and laborers as a way to discover a colleague's political allegiance or partying affiliation; *i.e. Hey everybody, it's 4:20... Let's get lit and read this shit!*

710 (7:10)- *n.* a term that is applied to all things cannabis concentrate, including the times at which it is appropriate everyday to dab; the concept comes from the fact that *710* spells out *OIL* upside down and reversed; also, *710* is the credit score of the average cannabis user

6630507 (US Patent 6630507)- *n.* the patent the US government holds on cannabis for its medical properties; allow me to point out that the US has classified cannabis as a Schedule I narcotic with no medical value and yet the government holds a patent on the medical properties of cannabis... yet another reason the US government is full of shit and should never be trusted; *see War on Drugs, The*

840 (8:40)- *n.* the stoner's 420, because no stoner is awake as early as 4:20; at *8:40*, one should consume twice as much cannabis for twice as long; the best way to start and end your day

1

absolute- *n.* a cannabis concentrate that has undergone a process to remove any fats, lipids, or plant waxes with a secondary solvent, specifically alcohol

Acapulco Gold- *n.* a legendary cannabis sativa landrace from the Acapulco region of Mexico

ACDC (AC/DC)- *n.* a sativa dominant cannabis strain that supposedly is a phenotype or hybrid of *Cannatonic* that was discovered and popularized by Dr. William Courtney from Northern California in his efforts to treat severely ill patients; *ACDC*'s claim to fame is that she is a strain with approximately a 20:1 ratio CBD to THC; rumor has it that *ACDC* got her abnormally high levels of CBD by being subjected to electroshock treatment, hence the name

acidic- *adj.* a term used to describe the relative acidity of a cannabis nutrient solution or growing medium; *see pH*

activist- *n.* one with little income or without a real job who is industrious in complaint and fastidious in being contrary to the status quo; in terms of cannabis, an *activist* is one who is a proponent for his own interpretation of legalization without regard for the needs of others, especially medical cannabis patients; *see legalization, decriminalization, reformer, Blue Ribbon Commission*

Adult Use of Marijuana Act (Control, Regulate and Tax Adult Use of Marijuana Act)- *n.* absurd, illogical, ridiculous bullshit written by people who seem to know dick about cannabis; even the name of the initiative is inaccurate (the word is cannabis, not marijuana, ignorant fucks); this trash legislation forces medical patients to be on a *voluntary patient registry* or pay recreational taxes on their medicine; it establishes and encourages local and county authorities to ban both recreational and medical cannabis while at the same time authorizing them to impose additional, obscene local taxes; furthermore, it taxes recreational cannabis twice, on wholesale and retail sales, doubling the likelihood that the average consumer won't pay the exorbitant price for legal cannabis; the fee schedule promises to be punitive and preventative, virtually ensuring a boom in an already dangerous and profitable black market; tell me, how the fuck is that possibly protecting the children?... oh, right, it's not... it's protecting your profits; your desire to get high and rich shall not come at the cost of medical cannabis patients and real California citizens; *i.e. I will not be voting to legalize recreational cannabis in California in 2016. The Adult Use of Marijuana Act, the most financially backed piece of legislation on the ballot, is also one of the most asinine. Unfortunately, too many special interest groups had their money involved in the construction of the language, and too few honest cannabis people were consulted. Now, if this shit passes, we're all fucked.; see marijuana, voluntary patient registry, reformer, Blue Ribbon Commission, legalization, possession limits, and Anslinger, Harry*

AE77 (AE77CaliO)- n. see California Orange

AEA- *abbrv. see anandamide*

aeration- *n.* the process by which air is introduced into, or made available in, a cannabis growing medium or nutrient solution; despite the common misconception by hydroponic growers who often water cannabis plants too frequently, cannabis roots need oxygen to thrive; thriving cannabis roots mean large, healthy cannabis plants, and *aeration* aids in dramatic root development; *aeration* is not to be confused with *blowing hot air,* which is what activists practice best

aeroponics- *n.* a type of cannabis cultivation where a nutrient solution is sprayed onto the cannabis roots inside a sealed reservoir

Afghani- n. an indica cannabis landrace originating from the Hindu Kush mountain range of Afghanistan

airplane- *n.* colloquial for cannabis based on the fact that it allows one to take flight with his feet firmly planted on the ground

air stone- *n.* a disc or ring typically made from porous volcanic rock that is attached to a pump and submerged into a reservoir in order to oxygenate a nutrient solution for hydroponic cannabis cultivation methods like nutrient film technique, aeroponics, and deep-water aquaculture

airy- *adj.* a term used to describe cannabis flowers that lack density or are light and leafy as opposed to tight, thick and chunky

AK-47- *n.* a sativa dominant cannabis strain bred by Serious Seeds that is a polyhybrid cross of *Columbian, Mexican, Thai, and Afghani; AK-47*'s notoriety stems from the supposition that she is a one-hit-wonder due to her strength; although selective breeding has created numerous contemporary strains that are significantly more potent than *AK-47*, the strain remains legendary

a little sumpin' sumpin' (a little sumpthin' sumpthin')- *phr.* a euphemism for fucking that has become a common colloquialism for cannabis, specifically fine-ass, juicy buds; *i.e. Hey girrrrl, le's get a little sumpin' sumpin' an den y'all cen give me somadat li'l' sumpthin' sumpthin', ya heard?*

all-purpose (all-purpose fertilizer)- *n. see generalized fertilizer*

alpha bisabolol- *n. see bisabolol*

alpha pinene- *n. see pinene*

aluminum pipe (aluminium pipe)- *n.* a type of pipe or smoking device that is constructed from aluminum; although there are conflicting scientific studies regarding the safe use of aluminum by humans, there is no reason to risk one's health by using an *aluminum pipe* to consume cannabis

amazon- *adj.* a juvenile colloquialism for extremely large cannabis flowers or plants; also, *amazon* can be used to describe voluptuous, curvaceous, leggy and sexy cannabis flowers

amendment (soil amendment)- *n.* a material added to a soil or soilless mixture in order to aerate or condition the medium, or to enrich it with nutrients or microbiologicals; some popular cannabis soil amendments include: alfalfa meal, bat guano, blood meal, bone meal, compost, crab meal, diatomaceous earth, dolomite lime, Epsom salts, feather meal, fish meal, green sand, gypsum, hemp protein powder, hulled hempseed, humic acid, insect frass, kelp, limestone, microbiologicals, mosquito prevention granules, mushroom compost, oyster shell meal, perlite, powdered molasses, pumice, recycled glass stones, reformer's bones, rock phosphate, silica, soybean meal, vermiculite, wood ashes, worm castings, and yucca

Amendment 64- *n.* the legislation in Colorado that legalized cannabis for adult recreational use

Americans for Safe Access- *n.* a cannabis organization whose founding principle is that all legitimate medical cannabis patients deserve the right to safe access to their medicine, not access from drug dealers on the street, or in shady, dirty, scary, *legal* dispensaries; although their efforts are to be commended, *Americans for Safe Access* has also greatly contributed to the false perception that there is a scarcity of CBD medicine with many of their scaremongering puff pieces on local dispensary owners who have been incarcerated for violating the laws in legal states

Amnesia Haze- *n.* a sativa dominant cannabis strain bred by Soma's Sacred Seeds that is a hybrid of *Afghani, Hawaiian, Southeast Asian* and *Jamaican* cannabis strains and landraces; what were we just talking about… I forgot

Amsterdam- *n.* a Dutch city in The Netherlands that is famed for its relatively loose cannabis laws and for its coffee shops that sell cannabis; *Amsterdam* was formerly the home of the High Times Cannabis Cup; due to legalization efforts in California, Colorado, and the United States, and the prejudice against dabbers and cannabis of the current Dutch government, the *Amsterdam* High Times Cannabis Cup was shutdown in 2015

anandamide- *n.* endogenous cannabinoid produced by the human body; *see cannabinoid*

ancillary cannabis products (ancillary goods)- *n.pl.* all products related to cannabis or cannabis cultivation that are not cannabis products themselves; *ancillary cannabis products* range from fertilizers to bags to bookkeeping services to this dictionary

Ani, Jennifer- *n.* a California attorney who specializes in protecting medical cannabis users' families from the persecution of Child Protective Services (CPS), and is noted for helping prevent CPS from abducting the children of legitimate medical cannabis patients

anointing oil (anointment oil)- *n.* the sanctified, Biblical oil used to consecrate the holiness of priests, kings, prophets and sacramental objects; the oil used to anoint Jesus, and possibly the oil Jesus used to anoint others; the recipe for *anointing oil* is clearly outlined in the Bible: extract six kilograms of myrrh, six kilograms of cassia, three kilograms of sweet cinnamon, and three kilograms of cannabis flowers into approximately seven liters of olive oil; the word *messiah* means *the anointed one* and directly refers to anyone blessed with *anointment oil*, especially Jesus; according to the Bible, it cannot be used to anoint *outsiders*, so I guess H.E. Hinton fans are out of luck

Anslinger, Harry- *n.* proof that Satan is real; the Pecksniffian poltroon and bigot responsible for the criminalization of cannabis in the US and, resultantly, the world; *Harry Anslinger* is famous for his witty and charming quotes on cannabis, like: "Reefer makes darkies think they're as good as white men."; *see coward asshole, marijuana, Adult Use of Marijuana Act*

6

anthocyanins- *n.pl.* a group of approximately four hundred water-soluble vacuolar pigments found in virtually all cannabis that can appear red, purple or blue depending on the pH of the medium; *anthocyanins* are classified as bioflavonoids or bioactive flavonoids and are extremely powerful antioxidants; in cannabis plants, *anthocyanins* are only visibly present in certain genotypes with high concentrations, or in genotypes with a cold-triggered genetic response that causes the appearance of the pigmentation like that of the retrotransponson activity in blood oranges

antiproliferative- *adj.* tending to or used to inhibit cell growth, specifically cancerous cell growth; one of cannabis' most authoritative benefits to humankind is its *antiproliferative* properties

apoptosis- *n.* the biological process of programmed or programmable cellular death; in terms of cannabis, *apoptosis* is the process cancerous cells in the human body undergo to destroy themselves upon introduction of high levels of THC and CBD; science has demonstrated though several studies that consumption of whole-plant cannabis and cannabis extracts can cause *apoptosis* of cancer cells, where the cells are literally reprogramed by the cannabinoids to commit suicide; *i.e. Her daily consumption of eight grams of oral cannabis flower contributed to the apoptosis of her melanoma.*

appellation- *n.* a legally designated geographical region that produces a specific agricultural crop; the title given to a legally protected agricultural region that is usually used to designate the origins of certain grapes (and the resulting alcoholic elixir, like *Champagne*), but has been applied to other crops; cannabis can, and should, be one of the crops to earn an *appellation* in a certain region; *i.e. After sampling the cannabis from the area, I see no reason why we should grant the San Joaquin Valley a cannabis appellation.; see outdoor*

apple pipe- *n.* a specific type of pipe made from an apple; a great MacGyver skill to have in case you need to smoke in a pinch; *i.e. You know what they say, "An apple pipe a day keeps the cancer at bay!"*

April 20th- *n.* the international cannabis holiday akin to St. Patrick's Day in that it is loosely based on a religious celebration and is centered around revelry in green; *see 420*

aquaculture- *n.* a type of hydroponic cannabis cultivation in which the roots are continuously submerged in a highly oxygenated, sterilized nutrient solution; certain *aquaculture* operations utilize active fisheries as the source for the nutrient solution

Arjan- *n.* the head breeder for Green House Seed Co. in Amsterdam; called the "King of Cannabis" and winner of over thirty-seven *High Times* Cannabis Cups; *Arjan* is responsible for some of the best cannabis ever bred, and some of the strangest; *see Green House Seed Co., Hawaiian Snow, Lemon Skunk, White Widow*

aroma- *n. see odor*

artisan cannabis- *n.* seemingly, the pretentious and erroneously egotistical term applied to small, usually poor or financially struggling, cannabis farms that have no real value or permanence other than a self-designated title… this is typically due to their inability to offer quality goods or an innovative strain or product instead of yet another *me, too*; in reality, anyone who cultivates as a passion, for cannabis and not for cash, and refrains from using toxic, cookie-cutter hydroponic or synthetic nutrients, is an *artisan cannabis* cultivator; *see me, too*

ASA- *abbrv. see Americans for Safe Access*

asexual propagation- *n. see cutting, tissue culture*

ash hit (ass hit)- *n.* the last hit of a bowl, so named due to the fact that it is comprised predominately of ash and ass instead of cannabis flower or concentrate; *i.e. I abhor taking the ash hit,* *especially at a party... an attentive host never knowingly lets his guests take an ash hit.*

ashy- *adj.* having the characteristics of ash or an ash hit

Asian-eyed- *adj.* a racist and derogatory term for squinty-eyed; *see squinty-eyed*

Ask Ed- *n.* a question and answer column in *High Times* during the 1980s and 1990s written by cannabis cultivation expert and author, Ed Rosenthal; a good number of self-proclaimed cannabis authorities owe their expertise to this man and his works

astronaut- *n.* one who is extremely high, so high that their profession exists only in outer space; *i.e. It doesn't take an astronaut to write a book on cannabis, but it sure helps.*

Attitude Seed Bank (The Attitude)- *n.* a UK-based cannabis seed bank that is known for shipping to countries worldwide; *The Attitude* seemingly has the largest selection of souvenir cannabis genetics available online

Aunt Mary- *n. see Mary Jane*

autobuddering- *n.* the state or quality of a concentrate changing texture over time due to changes in humidity or barometric pressure

autoflowering (auto-flowering)- *adj. see ruderalis*

auxin- *n.* a plant hormone found in the cannabis stem tip that promotes elongation and is partly responsible for the effect known as phototropism; synthetic and commercial fertilizers and hydroponic nutrients are often supplemented with *auxins* to stimulate elongation and growth

azos- *abbrv.* the nitrogen-fixing bacterium Azospirillum *brasilense* frequently used in outdoor cannabis cultivation and organic cloning

B-Real- *n.* the handle of rapper and actor Louis Freese who is best known as being the front man for the highly pro-cannabis rap group, Cypress Hill; *B-Real* is gaining recognition in the burgeoning cannabis industry as a crossover act who now collaborates with such groups as Humboldt Seed Organization to drop nuts to the world instead of rap cuts

B vitamins- *n.pl.* a group of vitamins often used in cannabis cultivation applications as *all-natural* root and growth stimulants; *B vitamins* benefit cannabis plants by assisting in healthy metabolic function, increasing immune response, aiding in the absorption and creation of carbohydrates, and, ultimately, increasing the overall final weight; those who refute the benefits of *B vitamins* quite possibly aren't fine-tuning their cannabis cultivation well enough to notice a difference; *B vitamins* are highly beneficial in the plant's development of roots and early growth, as well as being a great nutrient catalyst for explosive production at three of the major metabolic shifts during the life cycle of the cannabis plant: from seed to seedling, from seedling to sexually mature plant, and from vegetative growth into flowering; there are many organic, natural sources of *B Vitamins*, including brewer's yeast, hemp protein powder, and hulled hempseed

Bacillus *thuringiensis* (Bt, Bti, Btk)- *n.* a bacterium found in soil that is used in agricultural applications as a biological pesticide considered safe for humans and the environment; *Bacillus thuringiensis* is used to control many types of insects that lay their eggs and larvae in the soil, like fungus gnats, caterpillars, and mosquitos; *Bt* can be applied in liquid form, or as bits or granules

backcross (BX)- *v.* to pollinate a mother strain or plant with the pollen of an offspring, or vice versa, in order to breed back the traits of the original strain into a new generation of offspring; *i.e. I am trying to create an inbred backcross line of my Cali Lavender by pollinating an Old Lady Purp (Cali Lavender x Purple Dragon Kush) that represented like the mother with the last of the original male Cali Lav pollen.*

bag (baggie)- *n.* a quantity of cannabis; also, that in which cannabis is dispensed by the vast majority of dispensaries and dealers; albeit cheap, a *bag* is singularly one of the worst common ways to store or transport cannabis; any dispensary that administers cannabis flowers in zip seal *bags* purchased in bulk at the local big box store is a fucking joke… yeah, I said it: you're a loser if you sell cannabis in a plastic baggie; with another word preceding *bag*, it's the perfect description of many people in the cannabis industry

bag appeal (bag-appeal)- *n.* the overall size and attractiveness of a cured cannabis flower as it would be displayed in a baggie or jar; *bag appeal* is how posers grade cannabis; pretty does not mean potent or tasty; it's like the silicone laden bottle-blonde bud bimbos that would look better in a bag, because there's nothing of value inside anyway; give me a jar of party-bowl sized nugs, so I know that a half ounce is a half ounce, not a quarter bud and quarter stem; size does matter: big buds mean big stems

bag seed- *n.* the prize inside; a seed discovered in cannabis flowers purchased from a dispensary or dealer; often, though definitely not always, *bag seeds* are feminized selfed seeds created from pollen produced by the mother plant

bagtainer- *n.* a bag of soil that is designed to be used as the container for cultivating cannabis as well as that in which the soil is packaged; *for differentiation, see container bags*

bake- *v.* a colloquialism meaning to smoke cannabis; —*baked adj.* the characteristic or quality of having recently smoked cannabis; along the continuum, *baked* is an even spaced median between high and stoned, like being crispy on the outside and chewy in the middle; *i.e. I got so baked last night that I couldn't help but to bake some more!;* —*baker n.* one who *bakes* or otherwise smokes or vapes cannabis; the piece or implement through which one *bakes*; also, a *baker* occasionally refers to a joint or blunt

bale- *n.* a large compressed block or sack of exported cannabis equivalent to approximately thirty to one hundred kilos

ballast- *n.* the device that translates the electricity from a power source into useable electricity for horticultural lighting; there are two common types of *ballasts* used in indoor cannabis cultivation: *magnetic ballasts and digital or electronic ballasts*; both *ballast* types are employed in indoor cultivation, however digital *ballasts* are gaining popularity for their ease of use and reduced heat emissions; *i.e. He used four 1000-watt HPS fixtures on digital ballasts in his last indoor grow room.*

balls (big ol' balls)- *n.pl.* as in most species, *balls* are the male cannabis flowers, or hermaphroditic representation of male flowers on a female flower; what it takes to write a book like this

bamba- *n.* colloquial for cannabis

bammy- *n.* a variation of bamba; also, one who smokes bamba

banana- *n.* a single male cannabis anther or stamen appearing on or in a female cannabis flower; the presence of a *banana* indicates that a plant has undergone some stressor to trigger a hermaphroditic response in order to perpetuate the species; this trigger can be age, light fluctuation, nute burn, temperature, weak genetics or a specific strain's characteristic

Bangladesh- *n.* an indica cannabis landrace from Bangladesh; often used as a metaphor for one's aroma aura after smoking cannabis; *i.e. Shit, after blazing that bomb OG, I went to the 7-Eleven and people be peepin' me like I be smellin' like Bangladesh... It was cool as fuck, ya know what I'm sayin'!?!*

bank- *n. see seed bank;* also, a place that at present time cannot reap the financial rewards from the exploding cannabis industry... maybe if the bankers get upset enough at the billions and trillions of dollars they are potentially losing daily to the idiocy and hypocrisy of the federal government they will help get the laws changed

bans- *n.pl.* imposed restrictions, limitations or terminations to peoples' legal right to use medical or recreational cannabis in certain cities or counties in legal states; a way for small-time, ignorant public official tyrants to exercise their idiocy and bigotry; a way for board of supervisor members to earn hundreds of thousands of dollars under-the-table from black market and gang-run drug organizations as a means to prevent legal establishments from suctioning massive amounts of revenue from these illicit sources (thanks, fuckers); anyone with any semblance of intelligence can see through the lies of these politicians, and it is time we call out and boycott the cities and counties who are either intentionally or ignorantly murdering sick people by denying them their democratically voted right to use medical or recreational cannabis; *i.e. Counties like Tuolumne that have enacted cannabis bans deserve the poverty and intolerance their shortsightedness begets.*

Barney's Farm- *n.* a cannabis breeding company based in the Netherlands that is known for producing some truly unique, cup-winning strains, like *G13 Haze, Pineapple Chunk, Tangerine Dream, Cookies Kush, Sweet Tooth, Red Dragon, and Dr. Grinspoon*

basic- *adj.* a term used to describe the relative basicity of a cannabis nutrient solution or growing medium; *see pH*

bat- *n.* a specific type of one-hitter pipe that is shaped like a baseball bat and is often made from aluminum

bat guano- *n.* bat shit; *see guano*

batch test- *v.* to test multiple cannabis product or flower samples from a single harvest or batch to average for the purposes of determining the overall potency of said batch; —*n.* the testing procedure used to determine the overall average potency of a batch or harvest of cannabis; *i.e. I had SC Labs run a batch test on my Valhalla to determine how fuckin' badass she is.*

beach sand- *n. see sand*

beans- *n.pl.* colloquial for cannabis seeds; the term *beans* is most often used by immature and flatulent *breeders* stinking up the cannabis forums

bees hummin' in your ear- *phr.* paranoia; this is the sentiment popularized by Cypress Hill which suggests that the feeling of paranoia one experiences while high is similar to that of the anxiety experienced when having a bunch of *bees hummin' in your ear*

bejazzed- *adj.* a juvenile colloquialism for stoned, high or otherwise feeling the excited effects of cannabis consumption; possibly, this term stems from the similarities between the sensation of feeling *bejazzed* and the feeling of a *beejay; i.e. I'm fuckin' jazzed to be sittin' here bejazzed an' about t' jizz from getting' a beejay from my vajazzed girl, Jazz.*

bell- *n. see dome;* this is not to be confused with the curve on which prohibitionists reside firmly at the bottom left... the fact that 99% of the bigots will not understand this joke serves to acutely illustrate my point

belly button- *n.* a specific type of dome that sits adjacent to the nail, rather than covering it, for the vapor to be sucked in and through the rig reservoir and chamber; the *belly button* is named for its shape

beneficial bacteria- *n.pl.* the group of bacteria that colonize healthy soil, assist in chelation, and aid plants in the absorption of nutrients; *see microbiologicals, mycorrhizae*

beneficial insects- *n.pl. see beneficial predators*

beneficial predators- *n.pl.* organisms that aid in cannabis cultivation by destroying or neutralizing harmful insects and diseases; there are numerous *beneficial predators* successfully employed in the cannabis garden, including lady bugs, nematodes and praying mantises

bent- *adj.* stoned; in this case, if someone tells you to *get bent*, you can take it as a good thing; *i.e. I got fuckin' bent and listened to Elliphant's trippy shit... it's fuckin' bomb art, y'all.*

Berkeley- *n.* a city in California infamous for being a liberal, cannabis-friendly hub for hippies and stoners of all shapes, colors and sizes; many popular streets in *Berkeley* smell like human urine, which is possibly why they recently enacted city law that allows homeless people to get free medical cannabis from dispensaries

Berkeley Patients Group- *n.* the nation's longest continuously operating medical cannabis dispensary, located in Berkeley, California

beta caryophyllene- *n.* a common terpene found in cannabis that has a spicy aroma; as it is one of the primary medical constituents in cloves, rosemary and hops, *beta caryophyllene* has undergone numerous scientific studies that have determined its efficacy as an antidepressant and anxiolytic with neuroprotective and anti-alcoholism properties; *beta caryophyllene* is further proof that cannabis is indeed an invaluable medicine; *i.e. Patients looking to cure alcoholism might be interested in finding cannabis strains high in the terpene beta caryophyllene. It worked for me.*

bhang- *n.* ground or crumbled cannabis leaf and flower parts as opposed to *ganja*; often, *bhang* is ground into a fine powder, formed into a paste, and used in various foods; *bhang* is occasionally mixed with tobacco and kief and placed in the bowl of a hookah to smoke; also, *bhang* is used to name the milky drink made from cannabis; one could say that high quality cannabis is *bhangin'; for differentiation, see ganja*

BHO- *abbrv. see butane honey oil*

Bic- *n. see lighter*

biff- *n. see bliff*

Big Marijuana- *n.* a scaremongering moniker adopted by prohibitionists and cannabis reformers alike to define any large cannabis business or corporation; used as primary evidence against the argument for cannabis legalization; as if, somehow, a large cannabis conglomerate is in any way analogous with Big Tobacco… really?... alcohol and tobacco kill hundreds of thousands of people annually and cannabis can help people quit both without any risk of death, so maybe *Big Marijuana* is a lie invented by Big Alcohol and Big Tobacco that cannabis activists are too ignorant not to swallow whole like their precious pot brownies

binger- *n.* a bong; *i.e. Hurry up and bang that binger before I bong ya!*

biodynamic- *adj.* cannabis that has been grown using the *biodynamic* agriculture method

biodynamic agriculture (biodynamic gardening, biodynamic farming)- *n.* a method of organic farming that treats soil fertility, plant growth, and livestock care as inextricably connected as part of one fully functioning ecosystem; *i.e. The best cannabis I have ever experienced was grown in Santa Cruz County adhering to the precepts of biodynamic agriculture.*

bisabolol- *n.* a common terpene found in cannabis that has a slightly sweet floral aroma; as it is the primary medical constituent of German chamomile, *alpha bisabolol* has undergone numerous scientific studies that have determined its efficacy as an anti-inflammatory, antimicrobial, and anti-irritant known to cause apoptosis of leukemia cells; *bisabolol* is further proof that cannabis is indeed an invaluable medicine; *i.e.*

Patients looking to cure leukemia might be interested in finding cannabis strains high in the terpene alpha bisabolol.

black pepper- *n.* the spice, Piper *nigrum,* that supposedly counteracts the effects of paranoia that possibly stem from cannabis use; according to studies, the terpenes in common foods and herbs, like ginger, *black pepper* and mangoes, add to the entourage effect induced by whole-plant cannabis consumption; in the case of *black pepper*, the terpenes supposedly mitigate the anxiety occasionally induced by consumption of high levels of THC; *i.e. Legalization would be the best black pepper in the universe.*

black strap- *n. see molasses*

blast- *v.* to quickly saturate and then expel liquid butane or similar solvent through cannabis flowers or plant parts to extract the resin and create honey oil, wax or shatter; sadistic, unscrupulous demons *blast* fresh cannabis flowers to extract the resin and then sell the dried buds for normal price, doubling their profits

blasted buds- *n.pl.* cannabis flowers that have been run with a solvent and then dried and sold as acceptable cannabis; *i.e. The guy who sold me blasted buds from his dispensary is fucking lucky I'm not nineteen anymore.*

blaze- *v.* to spark a bowl; to burn a joint; to smoke cannabis; to publicly burn the name of a terrible dispensary that just sold you some shitty-ass cannabis

blazer- *n.* one who blazes; or, a joint, pipe, bong, blunt or other method of smoking cannabis; a *blazer* is not to be confused with a lightweight sports coat that only people on the list can wear

bleezy- *n.* colloquial for a blunt

bliff- *n.* colloquial for a blunt, specifically one smoked to the head; literally, *bliff* is a conjunction of *blunt* and *spliff*

bloodshot eyes- *n.pl.* a stereotypical side effect of ingesting cannabis due to an increase of blood flow and a reduction of inflammation in the body; the main reason certain eye drop brands remained in business throughout the last thirty years

bloom- *n.* the formula of hydroponic nutrient designed specifically for the flowering cycle, or that contains the macronutrients typically necessary for flowering cannabis that is used in conjunction with another formula or formulas in multi-part nutrient formulations; —*v.* to flower cannabis plants

Blueberry- *n.* an heirloom indica dominant cannabis hybrid out of Oregon and Northern California that is purported to be a polyhybrid of *Juicy Fruit, Purple Thai, and Afghani; Blueberry* was popularized in the late 1970s through the early 1980s, reaching her peak popularity in the mid to late 1990s; rumor has it that, due to numerous outdoor plantations of *Blueberry*, she is one of the first naturalized indica cannabis strains to the area and is notoriously hermaphroditic; the bred and released version of the original is by DJ Short and supposedly is improved; *Blueberry* is known for her true and authentic taste and aroma of blueberries and her subtle blue hues at the end of flowering; she is a parent of the world famous Santa Cruz, California-bred original *Blue Dream* strain

Blue Dream- *n.* a legendary sativa dominant hybrid that is *Blueberry* x an unknown *Haze,* most likely *Super Silver Haze; Blue Dream* is an amazing strain that truly tastes like California: bright, effervescent, floral and hazy blueberries, with a hint of sunshine and beautiful women that lingers like honey on your tongue upon exhale

Blue Ribbon Commission- *n.* a concerned group of citizens and *authorities* organized by California Lt. Governor Gavin Newsom; Newsom formed the *Blue Ribbon Commission* in order to investigate the impacts of cannabis legalization in California in 2016, and to report a *suggested* way for lawmakers and initiative writers to create legalization legislation; one of the primary findings of the commission is that California must find a way to prevent Big Marijuana from influencing politics like Big Alcohol and Big Tobacco; Mr. Burns... er... Mr. Nuisance and his wineries and bars obviously don't like healthy capitalist competition and therefore he must hate America; *i.e. The Blue Ribbon Commission was a joke, and it made findings based on information provided by people who know less about cannabis than an average thirteen-year-old. I believe it was just another way for prohibitionists to force influence on California reform groups too ignorant to see the truth... or too paid off to oppose the lies.*

blunt- *n.* one's truth about cannabis to the violent and vocal prohibitionist ignoramuses; a joint rolled with a tobacco wrapper instead of a paper; a *blunt* is the equivalent of a gorgeous woman wearing too much makeup, or a perfectly cooked Kobe beef fillet smothered in expired ketchup; —*blunted adj.* having the quality of being high or stoned off a blunt; more universally, *blunted* is used simply to mean lit the fuck up by any cannabis smoking, using any method of ingestion; contrary to popular belief, *blunted* is not a reference to cannabis users becoming more obtuse after consumption

bluntage- *n.* an indeterminate amount of cannabis flowers; *i.e. I had a hard-ass week, man. Let's get some bluntage and get posted up.*

Bluntage Road- *n.* a colloquial name for a road down which one might drive to pull over somewhere and smoke or use cannabis, based on its homophonic similarity to Frontage Road; *i.e. The other day we was parked over offa Bluntage Road, an' we saw some crazy-ass UFO shit. It was fucked!*

Bluntman and Chronic- *n. see Jay and Silent Bob*

blunt wrap- *n.* the tobacco wrapper used to roll a blunt; *blunt wraps* are often sold as such, already empty of the tobacco, but were originally removed from the inside of a cigar; traditionally, blunts were rolled with Philly brand cigars to make a *philly* or philly blunt, Dutch Masters to make a *dutchie*, or Swisher Sweets brand to make a *sweetie* or sweet blunt

bodega- *n. Spanish* a small grocery store, typically found in Hispanic boroughs on the East Coast, that has a reputation as being a place for one to illegally procure cannabis

Bodhi Seeds- *n.* a boutique breeding company that is responsible for developing some truly innovative cannabis hybrids available on the market; notably, *Bodhi Seeds* has some of the most unique and creative strain names, like *Dank Sinatra, Road Kill Unicorn, Elf Snack,* and *Dream Beaver,* to name only a few; also, Bodhi is famous for saying, "It's not how high you are; it's 'hi, how are you?'"

body high- *n.* the sensation one feels in her body after consuming cannabis, especially cannabis that is a heavy indica, high in CBD, or otherwise sedative or relaxing

bogart- *v.* to keep possession of a joint or smoking device while in the middle of a smoking session with others; usually, this is done for one of two reasons: the person is so fucked that they forget to pass that shit, or the jerk-off just wants to smoke all my bomb buds for free; supposedly, *bogart* comes from the cigarette smoking habits of Humphrey Bogart

bohippian- *n.* one who participates in the Bohippian Movement; literally, *bohippian* is a conjunction of *bohemian* and *hippie;* — *adj.* having the characteristics of a *bohippian* or of the Bohippian Movement; *see Bohippian Movement*

Bohippian Movement- *n.* a personal, philosophical and social movement that is founded on the principles of peace, unity, philanthropy and joy; tenets of the *Bohippian Movement* include a respect and equality for all people who choose to live in harmony with the world and others, and the precept that personal freedom begets mutual respect which begets mutual benefit; refraining from social media, alcohol consumption, elective plastic surgery, wanton internet engagement, and superfluous commercialism is a direct path to discovering personal freedom and therefore bohippians often are unplugged with the exception of basic utilities and a home phone line; furthermore, bohippians prefer the use of natural medicines and euphoriants, specifically and preferentially cannabis; they practice organic homesteading or eating with a focus on shopping locally and having as much of a *no murder* diet as possible; and they encourage an active lifestyle that includes gratuitous artistic expression; signifiers of the *Bohippian Movement* are people surrounded by positivity, fun music, bright colors and clouds of cannabis smoke; *i.e. The Bohippian Movement rocks! It is so much fun and a way more humanitarian philosophy to follow than Scientology or Catholicism.*

bolt- *n.* a large, thick joint; —*v.* to jump into flower prematurely; occasionally, when growing outdoors, cannabis will *bolt* if planted or germinated too early; *i.e. I rolled that schwag into a bolt and gave it away. It came from a plant that bolted.*

bomb (the bomb)- *n.* colloquial for potent, quality cannabis flowers; —*adj.* having the characteristics of *the bomb*; this term is so used due to the metaphorical effect that potent cannabis has on the minds of users

bomber- *n.* a large joint; *i.e. Let's get some bomb, juicy bomb and roll a big-ass bomber.*

bone- *n.* colloquial for a joint; *i.e. Hey, man, I gotta packa bones... wanna go for a ride and blaze?*

bong- *n.* a water-cooled pipe used to smoke cannabis; mistakenly considered the healthiest mode of cannabis inhalation; according to current research, the *bong* water filters out some of the beneficial cannabinoids and terpenes and leaves many of the tars to pass into the lungs; a *bong* is called a *water pipe* in headshops due to the idiocy of law, though I've never heard anyone say, *Yo! Stop bogartin' that shit. Hit the water pipe already, bro.*

bong hit- *n. see bong rip, hit*

bong load (bong-load)- *n.* the term applied to the variable amount of cannabis that can be loaded or packed into the bowl of a bong; also, *bong load* is used to quantify the total amount of cannabis consumed in a sitting as opposed to a single hit of cannabis; *i.e. Me an' my homeboy just sat there smokin' bong load after bong load while watching Pink Floyd's The Wall... talk about a mindfuck!; for differentiation, see bong rip*

bong lord- *n.* one who goes by the philosophy that he who holds the bong, owns the bong, or vice versa; typically, a *bong lord* is one who sits at the head of the table or the center of a gathering like a Don, packs a big-ass bowl that looks like it should be passed around, and then smokes the whole thing to his head while leaving everyone else to fend for himself; actually, he who controls the buds controls the bong; *i.e. Considering that I grew twenty-three different strains this season, I have a right to be the bong lord.*

bong rip- *n.* one hit or inhalation of cannabis smoke through a bong; also, an expulsion of flatulence that follows taking a huge *bong rip*; *i.e. After taking a big fat bong rip, I couldn't hold it in and had to let a bong rip out.*

bong water- *n.* the water or liquid used in the reservoir of a bong that the smoke is drawn through prior to being inhaled into the lungs; *bong water* emanates truly one of the most repulsive and unmistakable effluvia known to humans; although many cannabis smokers fail to adhere to this, the best advice is to change the *bong water* between each smoking session... and definitely don't drink that shit; *i.e. I smoke so much that I change the bong water at least five times a day.*

bottom buds- *n.pl.* the bottommost flowers on a mature cannabis plant; typically, *bottom buds* are of low or poor quality due to the fact that they are occluded or obscured from sunlight by the larger colas and upper buds; oftentimes, the phrase *bottom buds* is used to refer to any flower of low or poor quality

bottom shelf- *n.* the least expensive cannabis flowers on a dispensary menu, or the second least expensive if the dispensary has a house blend or compassion shelf; typically, the *bottom shelf* is comprised of outdoor cannabis, or subpar, dirty, or moldy indoor flowers; all *bottom shelves* are not created equally: there can be top-quality outdoor cannabis flowers on this shelf that are significantly better than the indoor samples simply because customers erroneously perceive outdoor cannabis to be of lower grade than indoor; *i.e. I find it crazy that they put your 27% THC outdoor nugs on the $200 bottom shelf when their house indoor only tests out at 16% THC and sits cozy on the top at $380 an ounce... I mean what the fuck, right?; for differentiation, see compassion shelf, top shelf; —bottom-shelf adj.* having the characteristic or quality of the *bottom shelf*

Boveda- *n.* a company that manufactures and sells humidipacks for use in long-term cannabis storage; in a sealed container, *Boveda* humidipacks can maintain the proper humidity to cure cannabis for up to a year

bowl- *n.* the receptacle at the top of a stem or in a pipe that holds cannabis for combustion and ingestion; a vague measurement of a consumable quantity of cannabis weighing roughly one quarter gram to one or more grams; *i.e. I smoked five bowls of that top-shelf schwag from Arnold, and all I got was a fucking headache. They're supposed to be the best? C'mon... LMFAO... maybe their bullshit buds are why the board is considering banning cultivation in the county!*

bowl filler- *n.* any low quality cannabis consumed simply for the effect, not the appreciation; said cannabis is put at the bottom of the bowl with a small portion of quality cannabis or cannabis concentrate placed on top to mindfuck oneself into believing that the entire bowl is the good shit; *bowl-filler* is comparable to cheap-ass mini-mart vodka being used as a mixer for a fine, aged scotch

bowl sparklers- *n.pl.* tiny, usually severely immature, cannabis seeds in a flower that has been packed and ignited; the moisture contained within the seeds immediately evaporates, causing a popping or sparking in the combusted material; *i.e. Oooo damn, check out those bowl sparklers! Where'd you get that shit, cuz? I wanna stay away from any place selling seedy schwag.; bowl sparklers* are not to be confused with the people to whom Jack Kerouac was referring in *On the Road*:

> *...because the only people for me are the mad ones, the ones who are mad to live, mad to talk, mad to be saved, desirous of everything at the same time, the ones who never yawn or say a commonplace thing, but burn, burn, burn, like fabulous yellow roman candles exploding like spiders across the stars and in the middle you see the blue center-light pop and everybody goes "Awww!"*

bowl topper- *n. see topper*

box (box out)- *v. see hot box*

Brave Mykayla- *n.* a brave young girl from Oregon who conquered childhood leukemia with the help of a cannabis oil treatment

Brazilian- *n.* a sativa cannabis landrace from Brazil; a beautiful cannabis flower that has been waxed clean of all leaves and left revealing the silken sexy shininess beneath; also, cannabis flowers that have been trimmed and stripped to prevent from spilling out of the folds

breed- *v.* to reproduce cannabis plants; to place male or feminized cannabis pollen on female cannabis flowers in order to create specific cannabis offspring in seed form

breed and select- *v.* to grow out offspring from two parents, select the best representations of the bunch, breed with those few, and then grow out the new offspring to select the best ones to do the process all over and over again until a cannabis strain has been stabilized or bred to the point of satisfaction

breeder- *n.* one who places male or feminized cannabis pollen on female cannabis flowers in order to create specific cannabis offspring in seed form; occasionally, this is the only form of sex being practiced by the *breeder*; *for differentiation, see pollen slinger*

breeder handle- *n.* the pseudonym a breeder assumes in public in order to preserve her anonymity or privacy; *i.e. Once I realized the idiocy of a breeder handle, I dropped the "Sage" and started using my real name. A wise decision now, I imagine.*

breeder pack- *n.* a sealed pack of seeds originating from the breeder or breeding company*; i.e. I got my wife a breeder pack of Power Kush as a stocking stuffer.*

breeding company- *n.* a company whose sole purpose is to create and sell cannabis genetics, usually comprised of legitimate breeders (but not always); most breeding companies are run by decent enough people, but some actually have the audacity and sadism to charge $250-$1000 for a single breeder pack of ten seeds... as a legitimate breeder let me say this to those assholes: your shit isn't that good, it's not rare or high end (no matter what you try to convince yourselves), and no honest or compassionate person would ever fathom charging that much money for MEDICAL CANNABIS genetics... you heartless, self-indulgent pricks; also, many *breeding companies* are actually clothing and apparel businesses on the books, and are possibly guilty of serious federal tax crimes; *i.e. In this day and age, everyone can see through the tax fraud and money laundering of illegitimate, trashy breeding companies.;* regardless of the current population of the cannabis breeding community, *breeding companies* and breeders deserve our respect and gratitude for providing so many beneficial and varied strains to the public and for keeping heirlooms alive during prohibition

brick- *n.* a large chunk or block of compressed cannabis that typically weighs one kilo; adds new meaning to *brick*-and-mortar dispensary; *i.e. I once saw a whole brick in person and the experience reminded me of seeing a celebrity in real life: it was* *much smaller and didn't look nearly as good as it did in photographs.*

brick-and-mortar- *n.* a cannabis dispensary in a legal and legitimate physical location as opposed to a drug delivery service; thanks to the government, where you will find the remains of many early cannabis activists, reformers and pioneers

brick bud- *n. see Mexican brick bud*

broccoli- *n. see veggies*

brownie- *n. see magic brownie*

Bubba Kush- *n.* an indica dominant cannabis hybrid that is *OG Kush x West Coast Dog x Old World Kush* and was clone-only prior to 1998; since then, many people have released S1s or knockoffs under the name *Bubba Kush*, but supposedly these are not in fact the real *Bubba Kush;* nowadays, *Bubba Kush* ain't *Bubba Kush* unless she's *pre '98 Bubba Kush*

bubble- *n. see bubble hash*

bubble bags- *n.pl.* the screened bags used in the production of bubble or ice water hash

Bubble Gum (Bubblegum)- *n.* a legendary indica dominant cannabis hybrid originally from Indiana that was released in seed form by Serious Seeds; *Bubble Gum* gets her name from the fact that she unmistakably tastes like sweet pink bubblegum

bubble hash- *n.* a specific style of hash that is made by carefully churning cannabis flowers or parts in ice water to loosen the glandular trichomes, and then filtering the spent water through screened bags in order to separate the glands and resins from the liquid

bubble machine- *n.* a small, portable clothes washing machine that has been slightly altered in order to agitate cannabis parts for the purpose of making bubble hash; in reality, a *bubble machine* simply mixes the ice, cannabis, and water, and the hashmaker still needs to do the tedious and time-consuming process of filtering and straining the hash

bubbler- *n.* a specific type of water pipe that has a continuous construction as opposed to a bong that has removable parts like a bowl, stem and slide; this term can also mean one who smokes a large quantity of bubble, like the pothead equivalent for hash smokers; *i.e. The bubbler likes to smoke all that hash out of a bubbler.*

bubonic (bubonic chronic)- *n.* a colloquialism for chronic based on the fact that an overwhelming sense of paranoia can plague a person after the consumption of cannabis

bud- *n. see buds*

bud and breakfast- *n.* a bed and breakfast in a legal state that caters to, or is friendly to, cannabis users; *i.e. It would be kick-ass if they turned that place in Carmel into a bud and breakfast.*

bud bimbos- *n.pl.* the group or groups of women who parade around the social media and forums in their panties or pussies pretending to smoke cannabis; there are numerous, organized brands of *bud bimbos* that will remain unnamed due to legal backlash from the gash; these women are also endearingly and honestly referred to as ganja girls, cannabis coquettes, weed whores and canna cunts; *bud bimbos* make themselves look trashy, trampy and toasty, and are yet another filthy symptom of the socially transmitted disease overwhelming the world known as narcissism; *bud bimbos* are not to be confused with the *social media bikini warriors* who are a similar group of sluts and prostitutes but who refrain from adding cannabis to their boudoir; *for differentiation, see goo goo doll*

bud density- *n.* the loosely quantifiable signifier for the relative weight of a cannabis flower to the amount of space it takes up; the density of a cannabis flower; *i.e. Bud density is only one of* *several factors used to determine the quality of a cannabis flower.*; *bud density* is not to be confused with the relative intelligence quotient of your best friend

bud leaf- *n. see sugar leaf*

bud sites- *n.pl. see node*

bud structure- *n. see flower structure*

budder (budda)- *n.* a specific type of solvent-extracted concentrate that is similar to wax, but more oily and less crumbly; what cigarette smokers and meth heads cough up from their lungs

budder-faced- *adj.* the dabber's equivalent to stoned or high; or, what happens to a bud bimbo at a party, like Bukake

Buddha (buddha)- *n.* colloquial for top quality cannabis

budding- *adj. see flowering*

buds- *n.pl.* dried or cured cannabis flowers; green gold; people who should never know where your garden grows

Buds and Roses- *n.* the popular Southern California dispensary that earned its fame by winning cups with, and offering for sale, Kyle Kushman's veganic cannabis and ancillary cannabis products

budtender (bud tender)- *n.* a somewhat derogatory term for a medical cannabis administrator; acceptable and appropriate term for adult legal-use disseminators in establishments that sell cannabis flowers; *budtender* is not to be confused with the exorbitant cost paid for cannabis flowers

buffer- *n.* a substance that prevents fluctuation; in cannabis cultivation, a *buffer* is typically an amendment like lime or oyster shell meal that prevents a medium from becoming too acidic

buildup- *n. see salt buildup*

bunk- *n.* terrible quality cannabis; —*adj.* having the quality of *bunk* cannabis; *i.e. She brought me over some bunk from Escalon. It was as bunk as Quail Valley schwag, so we kicked her cracker ass out the party.*

burn- *v.* to combust cannabis, often used specifically to describe smoking a joint; *i.e. Let's go burn one in the girls bathroom.*

burned Bic bottom- *phr.* the phrase used to describe finding out that someone you least expect is a cannabis smoker; *i.e. To my surprise, my boss had a burned Bic bottom… so, I took her out after work to smoke a buncha bowls.;* the term comes from the fact that many people who carry a lighter and smoke cannabis from a pipe or bong often use the bottom of their lighter to tamp out the cherry; *i.e. I turned over her burned Bic bottom and tamped the fuck out of her cherry. I guess you could say that I was tappin' that ash.*

burner- *n.* one who burns; or, a joint, pipe, bong, blunt or other method of burning cannabis; a *burner* is not to be confused with a shart after eating habaneros

burnout- *n.* the derogatory term used by octogenarians and prohibitionists to describe one who has withdrawn from society, dropped out of school, or lost his job because of smoking that there devilweed; *i.e. The burnout stereotype is perpetuated by the marginally presentable and classless cannabis figureheads celebrated by the media moguls of the industry. If this weren't the case, why would a certain stoner rag give an innovation award to a teacher who publicly admitted smoking pot on school grounds while children were present? Fucking tacky. Pieces of shit like him are making us all look bad.*

burnt- *adj.* the state or condition of having just burned one or otherwise smoked or vaped some cannabis; *i.e. I smoked some shit with Jade and have never been so fuckin' burnt.*

30

burp- *v.* to periodically open a jar of cannabis flowers in order to release the last bits of moisture; *burping* is one of the last remaining steps before cannabis flowers are ready to be cured

butane- *n.* a fuel used in lighters and as a solvent to extract aromatic resins, glandular trichomes and active cannabinoids from cannabis flowers; explosive poison; additives in butane can cause cancer and other serious conditions if consumed for long periods of time or in large amounts, and are present in at least trace quantities of nearly all solvent-extracted cannabis concentrates (and even in many that claim to be solvent-less); most often, the *butane* used in concentrate making is a mix of *butane* and propane; *see purge*

butane honey oil (BHO)- *n.* a form of cannabis concentrate specifically made by blasting cannabis material with butane to create a honey-colored, oily extract

butter (cannabis butter)- *n.* a cannabis-infused butter typically used in cooking; *cannabis butter* has been replaced in more progressive and healthy circles; a good chef can get all the flavor and mouth feel of *butter* from organic plant oils, like coconut and red palm, without the detrimental side effects of the butter, like heart disease and obesity; *for disambiguation, see budder*

BX- *abbrv. see backcross*

31

cadet- *n. see space cadet*

cage- *v.* to surround a cannabis plant with fencing in order to keep the branches and colas supported; *caging* is often done in conjunction with trellis gardening or screen of green; *see screen of green*

Cali- *abbrv.* California; to where me 'n' LL be goin' back

calibration solution- *n.* the liquid with a set pH, EC or TDS that is used to set or regulate hydroponic solution testers and meters

California Orange- *n.* an old school cannabis heirloom hybrid out of California that dates back to the hippie era; in the 1980s, Dutch breeders, such as Sensi Seeds and Dutch Passion, preserved the strain in seed form and is still available to this day; one of *California Orange's* claims to fame is her notably bright, pungent, sweet-orange aroma; come to California and get the big O

CaliO (Calio)- *n. see California Orange*

camphor- *n.* a common terpene found in cannabis that has a sharp aroma; as it is one of the primary medical constituents of certain laurel trees, rosemary and certain basils, *camphor* has undergone numerous scientific studies that have determined its efficacy as an antimicrobial localized anesthetic; *camphor* is further proof that cannabis is indeed an invaluable medicine

cane- *n.* a large cola or spear of cannabis flowers, usually already dried and manicured; *for differentiation, see fragrant cane*

canister- *n.* a container similar to a jar but constructed of different materials or in a different shape that is used to store larger amounts of cannabis; the most common cannabis-specific *canisters* available are *CVaults*, which are stainless steel air-tight containers designed to be used in conjunction with humidipacks

canna— *prefix* the latest letter chain to be added to the illustrious list of English prefixes; in the cannabis industry, *canna* is the scapegoat moniker used by those lacking in creativity; *i.e. Did you see that new place opening up? Why would they name a pet food store, CannaCat? Isn't The Dank Dawg a better name?*

cannabichromene (CBC)- *n.* a nonpsychoactive cannabinoid with neuroregenerative, antiproliferative, analgesic, anti-inflammatory, and bone stimulating properties; patients use strains high in *cannabichromene* to combat bone-decay diseases like osteochondritis dissecans and osteoporosis; CBC: Cannabis Begets Compassion

cannabichromic acid (CBCa)- *n.* the precursor to cannabichromene with antifungal and anti-inflammatory properties

cannabicyclol (CBL)- *n.* a cannabinoid with anti-inflammatory and antimicrobial properties

cannabidiol (CBD)- *n.* amazing medicine; a nonpsychoactive cannabinoid with antipsoriatic, analgesic, anxiolytic, antipsychotic, antiepileptic, neuroprotective, vasorelaxant, antispasmodic, anti-ischemic, antiproliferative, antiemetic, antibacterial, antidiabetic, intestinal anti-prokinetic, bone stimulant, immunosuppressive, and anti-inflammatory properties; I list the last one to highlight its importance: cannabis can un-inflame your body and culture; *cannabidiol* has gained immense contemporary popularity, especially among parents, for its ability to SAFELY treat severe childhood diseases, like epilepsy; CBD: Cannabis Beats Degeneration

cannabidiolic acid (CBDa)- *n.* the precursor to cannabidiol and one of four possible derivatives of cannabigerolic acid (CBGa); after decarboxylation, cannabidiolic acid becomes cannabidiol

cannabidivarin (CBDv)- *n.* a cannabinoid with anticonvulsant and bone stimulant properties

cannabielsoin (CBE)- *n.* the cannabinoid metabolite of CBD

cannabigerol (CBG)- *n.* a nonpsychoactive cannabinoid with analgesic, antibacterial, bone stimulant, and anti-inflammatory properties; the metaphorical *stem cell* of cannabinoids, as it is the precursor to the other major cannabinoids like THC and CBD; *cannabigerol* could be the key to curing all illness, and is what scientists should research instead of human stem cells; why cannibalize when you can *cannabowlize?*

cannabigerolic acid (CBGa)- *n.* the precursor to cannabigerol with analgesic, anti-inflammatory, and antimicrobial properties

cannabinoids- *n.pl.* a group of approximately one hundred and eleven terpenophenolic compounds present in cannabis that bind to receptors in the body and occur naturally in the nervous and immune systems of humans and animals; there are three general types of *cannabinoid*: *phytocannabinoids* that occur uniquely in the cannabis plant; *endogenous cannabinoids* that are produced in the bodies of humans and other animals; and poisonous *synthetic cannabinoids* that are similar *man*-made compounds produced in a laboratory with severe and extreme side effects (I say *man* here not to be politically incorrect, but to illustrate that most often women aren't stupid enough to try to improve upon Mother Nature/God, unless it's fuckin' their bodies and faces up through plastic surgery)

cannabinoid profile- *n. see total cannabinoid profile*

cannabinol (CBN)- *n.* a mildly psychoactive compound created by the degradation of THC that has analgesic and slight immunosuppressive properties; highly narcotic and appetite stimulating; immediate hunger followed by sleep is often the result of *cannabinol* ingestion; some chemotherapy or other patients may choose to let their meds degrade just to have more *cannabinol*; the cannabinoid partially responsible for the stereotypical *stoned* feeling and stoner traits such as the munchies and couchlock (along with terpineol, myrcene, and

THC to a certain extent)

Cannabis- *n.* the perfect plant; the perfect medicine, food, fuel, and textile; the chink in the armor of their lies; a genus of nutritional and medical flowering plants divided into one species with three subspecies, Cannabis *indica*, Cannabis *ruderalis*, Cannabis *sativa* (low THC hemp is commonly classified as Cannabis *sativa L.; see hemp);* sometimes, *Cannabis* is divided into one species with two subspecies (Cannabis *sativa* subsp. *indica* or *spontanea*), but this is commonly considered inaccurate; recently, the taxonomic nomenclature of *Cannabis* classification was called into question, examined and "corrected" by John McPartland and Dr. Geoffrey Guy using DNA testing technology; their taxonomy of *Cannabis* is Cannabis *afghanica* (formerly C. *indica*), Cannabis *indica* (formerly C. *sativa*), and Cannabis *sativa* (formerly C. *ruderalis*), and has yet to be widely accepted; *Cannabis* is indigenous to all continents; its safe use as food, medicine and entertainment has been reported for over 10,000 years, and documented in writing as early as 2900 BCE; biblical figures, including Jesus, used cannabis and its extracts; the true anointment oil was predominantly an extract of *fragrant cane*, also known as *cannabis*; in organic flower form or as a chemical-free extract, it is safe for all humans of all ages to use; *i.e. Science has repeatedly demonstrated that humans cannot realistically overdose on cannabis, only on the solvents, fuels, and nutrients used to process and grow it.; for differentiation, see hemp, indica, sativa, ruderalis*

cannabis breathalyzer- *n.* currently a myth; *see per se DUI laws*

cannabis business- *n.* any legal, licensed business involved in cannabis cultivation, production, processing, transportation, storage, packaging, distribution, exchange, or sales including but not limited to bud and breakfasts, cannabis extraction facilities, cannabis farms, cannabiseries, grocery stores selling cannabis, hookah bars, medical cannabis pharmacies, operations, organizations, recreational cannabis facilities, restaurants, or yoga studios

cannabis clowns- *n.pl.* the industry term for people who pose, play, dabble, shit-talk instead of walk, or interlope in the cannabis community or industry instead of actually learning, knowing, and doing; weed nerds, dank dorks, dub doofs, ganja goofs, pot playas; *i.e. I am tired of these cannabis clowns talkin' all this shit on the facebook and in the forums when they don't know dick about cannabis, nor about me and my skills.*

cannabis cup- *n.* a state-fair-style competition for cannabis flowers, concentrates, edibles, and ancillary goods; famous *cannabis cups* include: the High Times Cannabis Cup, the High Times Medical Cannabis Cup, the Caregiver's Cup in Colorado, the Emerald Cup in California and the Oregon Medical Cannabis Awards; there are so many jokes here, I don't know where to begin... *grandma and Aunt Bea would be so proud... can we enter our prized pot pickle recipe, too?; so, I've heard it's as easy as buying a win or paying people to like you at the Emerald Cup... just ask Sean Parker and Tim Blake; if there's an accident at a cannabis cup, does it all go up in smoke?...* okay, enough...

cannabis fingerprint- *n.* according to current science, a *cannabis fingerprint* is the unique, never changing, exactly-the-same-always-without-any-adjustment-for-degradation terpene profile of a cannabis strain; I hate to call this pseudoscience into question, but any cannabis cultivator knows from their nose that a strain's terpene profile is not a stable entity; dollars to doughnuts, if one were to take the *cannabis fingerprint* of one strain at the time of first dry, and then perform the same test on the same specimen a month later, the fingerprints would be different

cannabis-infused- *adj.* having the quality of a consumable that has been enriched with vitamin cannabis or cannabis extracts; edibles, topicals and even smokeables can be *cannabis-infused*

cannabis-infused oil- *n.* the result of soaking, sautéing, or macerating cannabis flowers or plant parts in a culinary or cosmetic carrier oil such as apricot, avocado, coconut, olive, red palm, or sweet almond; *for differentiation, see oil, full extract cannabis oil, honey oil, concentrates*

cannabis lab- *n.* the facility in which cannabis lab testing occurs

cannabis lab test- *v.* to test cannabis samples in a laboratory; — *n.* the practice of testing cannabis and cannabis product samples to determine their potency or relative safety in regards to molds and bacteria or residual solvents; *i.e. In this day and age, any dispensary that fails to offer patients medicine that has undergone cannabis lab testing is cheap, lazy or shady.*

cannabis sap- *n.* the raw, viscous and nutritious extrusion of resins from a cut or cuts on, or through the expressing of, live or fresh harvested cannabis stems that can possibly be used as a natural sweetener; *for differentiation, see sap*

cannabis startup- *n.* a new cannabis business, specifically one in a province where cannabis has been legalized or decriminalized; *i.e. In this exploding time of legalization in the US and the world, thousands of classy and legitimate people are opening cannabis startups. It's about time we raised the (hash) bar on the quality of our company.*

cannabis tabs- *n.pl. see tabs*

cannabis yoga (yoganja)- *n.* a flexible spiritual enlightenment; a warm up routine for smokin' sex

cannabisery- *n.* a cannabis business that cultivates, processes, and packages recreational cannabis for retail sale or wholesale distribution and maintains a public cannabis tasting room analogous with a wine tasting room at a winery

cannanewbie- *n.* one who is new to the cannabis industry or to cannabis use; *cannanewbie* was formerly known as cannabis *virgin*, but this term is no longer in vogue due to the cultural extinction of the aforementioned species

Cannatonic- n. a sativa dominant cannabis strain bred by Resin Seeds that is *MK Ultra x G13 Haze*; purportedly, *Cannatonic* was the first commercially available strain high in CBD; *see cannabidiol*

cannoli- *n.* a specific preparation of bubble hash where the hash is pressed and rolled by hand to form the shape of an Italian cannoli; the *cannoli* is the flagship of hashmaker Frenchy Cannoli

caps (cannabis caps)- *n.pl.* the term applied to the group of cannabis edibles that are administered in capsules instead of brownies or candy; a mature edible; a smooth transition for cannanewbies accustomed to pharmaceutical use; typically, *caps* are filled with decarboxylated cannabis concentrate or cannabis flowers and occasionally a small amount of a fat, like coconut oil

capsules- *n.pl. see caps*

carb- *n.* a hole in a pipe, bong or other smoking or vaping device that is manually plugged with the hand or finger in order to complete the closed loop vacuum system that occurs when drawing in a hit of cannabis smoke; the *carb* is released to break the loop and cause the smoke to *pop* into one's lungs; occasionally, the *carb* will be referred to as the *bong hole*, but too many novice smokers get confused and mistake other people for instructing: "Plug the bunghole! Stick your thumb in the bunghole to carb it."

carb cap- *n.* a type of covered dome or globe used with a dab rig; *see dome*

carb load (carb loading)- *v.* to feed cannabis plants high doses of carbohydrates in order to stimulate or trigger specific biological responses in the plant or in the symbiotic microbiologicals in the medium; *see carbohydrates*

carbohydrates- *n.pl.* when it comes to cannabis, *carbohydrates* are the various sugars fed to plants; these *carbohydrates* stimulate certain hormonal production in cannabis, but mostly feed the mycorrhizae and beneficial bacteria to enhance their reproduction, which ultimately supercharges their chelating abilities and ups the availability of nutrients in the medium for immediate plant absorption; *carbohydrates* are often used as a flushing or finishing agent, however this must be done earlier than the typical flush or it will cause the opposite of the desired effect: the microbiologicals in the soil will chelate the nutrients, and the plant will absorb them right before harvest... this results in harsh cannabis, and is one of the follies of many self-proclaimed cannabis cultivating experts and weed nerds; when using *carbohydrates* for cannabis, it is best to select from a variety, and to use them only at the major metabolic growth shifts and during early and peak flowering; some optimal organic *carbohydrates* for use on cannabis are: agave, barley malt syrup, brown rice syrup, brown sugar, coconut nectar, coconut palm sugar, honey, maple syrup, and molasses

carbo load- *n.* the large dose of carbohydrates used to feed cannabis plants

carbon dioxide (CO2)- *n.* a gas that can be liquid at cold and pressurized situations, or a solid in subfreezing temperatures, that is broadly used in cannabis cultivation and processing; in cannabis cultivation, *carbon dioxide* is often supplemented in indoor operations with propane burners called *CO2* generators; in cannabis concentrate making, *carbon dioxide* is used in the form of a liquid gas to wash or bathe cannabis parts inside a specialized, pressurized machine in order to create *CO2* oil; also, solid *CO2* in the form of dry ice is used to separate kief from cannabis flowers by shaking the two together in a bubble bag or similar apparatus

carbon filter- *n.* a specific type of odor control constructed from a filter tube filled with activated carbon that is attached to the HVAC or ventilation and exhaust system in an indoor grow op or greenhouse; *see odor control*

carbs- *abbrv. see carbohydrates*

caregiver- *n.* one who is legally allowed to provide or procure medical cannabis for a verified medical cannabis patient, or patients, but who cannot provide cannabis for himself

cashed- *adj.* having the characteristic of an ash hit or finished bowl of cannabis; —*to cash v.* to finish a bowl or to dump the remains of a finished bowl prior to packing a new one; *i.e. Hey, Jonny, cash that bowl cuz that ash is cashed and my stash is too fat to smoke that shat.*

Cashmere- *n. see Kashmir*

caviar- *n.* cannabis flowers that have been dipped or coated in cannabis oil or hash and rolled in kief; a great method of pawning off cheap, low-quality cannabis and cannabis extracts to wide-eyed cannanewbies at $1000-$1500 an ounce; it is fairly easy to take bottom buds, coat them in leaf or trim oil, and roll them in stem kief to create pretty trash and call it *caviar*

CBC- *abbrv. see cannabichromene*

CBCa- *abbrv. see cannabichromic acid*

CBD- *abbrv. see cannabidiol*

CBDa- *abbrv. see cannabidiolic acid*

CBDv- *abbrv. see cannabidivarin*

CBE- *abbrv. see cannabielsoin*

CBG- *abbrv. see cannabigerol*

CBGa- *abbrv. see cannabigerolic acid*

CBL- *abbrv. see cannabicyclol*

CBN- *abbrv. see cannabinol*

CCREAM- *acronym* the phrase used to identify our current economy, classify our social priorities, and revere our communal deity: *cannabis cash rules everything around me*

Cervantes, Jorge- *n.* a popular cannabis cultivation guru and author; *Cervantes* was Ed Rosenthal's replacement for the grow column in *High Times Magazine*

Chamba- *n. see Malawi*

chamber- *n.* the part of a bong or pipe that is filled with cannabis smoke prior to inhalation into the lungs; I wonder if this is the *chamber* to which Emily Dickinson was referring when she proclaimed of her imaginary friend:

> *Reaching late his flower,*
> *'Round her chamber hums—*
> *Counts his nectars—*
> *Enters—and is lost in Balms.*

charas- *n.* a specific type of hand-rolled hash, typically finger hash, from India

Charlotte's Web- *n.* a high CBD, sativa dominant cannabis strain made available to the public (for a price) in Colorado by the Stanley Brothers; although they claim to be the breeders, as of this time, they supposedly have not yet released a cutting for comparison to Dr. Courtney's *ACDC*; a popular belief is that the Stanley Brothers purportedly worked with a cutting of Dr. Courtney's *ACDC* and renamed her *Charlotte's Web* to use in their breeding programs; the strain gets her moniker from Charlotte Figi, a young child with epilepsy, who popularized the plant in her battle with the disease

cheap high- *n.* one who requires very little cannabis in order to feel its effects; a financially impossible state of being for any cannabis user other than an abstainer; *i.e. I have never been accused of being a cheap high.*

cheeba- *n.* a Brazilian word for cannabis that is used colloquially worldwide

Cheech and Chong- *n.* cannabis legends and icons, Cheech Marin and Tommy Chong, immortalized for their cannabis-centered films and records; *see Chong, Tommy*

Cheese (Exodus Cheese)- *n.* a *Skunk* cultivar discovered in the UK that gets its name and infamy from the fact that the flowers unmistakably smell like asiago or limburger cheese; —*adj.* having the characteristic of my jokes

chelate- *v.* to form a *chelate* with, or to undergo the process to form a *chelate*; —*n.* in layman's terms, a *chelate* is a necessary mineral or nutrient that has undergone a natural process in order to make it biologically available for absorption by plant roots; *i.e. The pH of a medium will become more acidic as the organic amendments decompose and the nutrients they contain begin to chelate; therefore, it is advised to control for this by applying an organic soil conditioner that is basic, like oyster shell meal or limestone.*

Chemdog- *n.* the handle of the person who found the *Chemdog* 1-4 bag seeds, arguably one of the most unique unknown hybrid strains of cannabis; *Chemdawg-4* [sic], the seed that supposedly best represented the original bag, smells more like burning chemicals than cannabis, and is one of the greatest strains currently available (that's #4, not #3 or '91; those two pale in comparison to #4 and are relatively ordinary); the *Chemdog* line is supposedly the parent to such famous strains as *Sour Diesel, ECSD, OG Kush;* —*chemdog n.* a derogatory term for a cannabis gardener who relies solely on poisonous hydroponic nutrients for cannabis cultivation; *i.e. That Modesto grower must be a chemdog. I smoked his Chem '91 and nearly hacked up a bloody lung.*

cherry- *n.* the lit tip of a joint or a bowl of cannabis that is smoldering or coaled; *i.e. Here, here… hit this shit while there's* *a cherry.;* also, *cherry* is still the euphemism for one's virginity: in this case, popping the cannabis *cherry* involves a really hot cherry; —*cherried adj.* having the characteristic of a *cherry*

Chetrar- *n. see Chitral*

chief- *v.* an insensitive and racist colloquialism for bogart; *i.e. Maybe cannabis people would earn more respect if they would cease being so bigoted, dontcha think there, chief?; see bogart*

Chilean Miners- *n.pl.* the group of thirty-three men who were trapped in a mine for over two months in 2010; when they emerged, all the men were alive, fairly healthy, and relatively happy; this miracle is due in no small part to the fact that they were provided and prescribed a specific, supposedly organic, diet that included the smoking of cannabis; it is my humble belief as a five-year-sober alcoholic that they would all have killed each other had they been provided booze instead of cannabis

chill- *v.* to relax and consume cannabis without any worry or stress; —*adj.* having the characteristic or quality of one who *chills*; also, *chill* can be used synonymous with baked or, occasionally, stoned; *i.e. My love and I dig chillin' with bud like Candy Girl that makes us feel real chill.*

chillin' on the moon- *phr.* the description of being high or chill after or while consuming cannabis

chill pill- *n.* a colloquial term originating in the American idiomatic vernacular that now applies to cannabis capsules, hash caps, cannabis mints or dissolvable cannabis tabs; the term has since been adopted as a product name by a company in Colorado, but they cannot trademark public domain as their own… or sure as shit shouldn't be able to

chillum- *n.* a straight pipe smoking device that originated in India and South America (supposedly independently); typically, the *chillum* is used in ceremonial or religious celebrations involving the ingestion of sacred cannabis; what happens to numerous first-time cannabis users: they get really *chill* and all they can say is *um*

Chinese-eyed- *adj. derogatory see Asian-eyed*

Chiquita Banana- *n.* a phenotype of the indica dominant cannabis strain *Banana Kush* bred by Crockett Family Farms that is *Ghost OG x Skunk Haze*; predictably, *Chiquita Banana* smells and tastes like overripe bananas; notably, this trendy strain has repeatedly tested at over 30% THC… there's no putting a condom on a high like that; *i.e. Don't get caught slippin' on that Chiquita Banana, yo.*

Chitral (Chetrar)- *n.* a village district in the Hindu Kush mountains of Pakistan where the *Chitral* indica cannabis landrace originated; *for disambiguation see Citral, Citralah*

chlorosis- *n.* the condition in cannabis cultivation that becomes a plant that is deprived of nitrogen or iron and is the result of the microbiologicals robbing nutrients from the medium; in early growth through mid-flowering, *chlorosis* is a sign of problematic nutrient deficiency; however, it is a natural and necessary part of the ripening process in properly fed cannabis and should be viewed as a great sign when it appears during the last ten to fourteen days of flowering as it is visible proof of a plant being depleted of excess nutrients

Chocolate Thai- *n.* a sativa dominant cannabis heirloom strain from Thailand that was bred for generations to represent with an incredible aroma of chocolate and hash, or dark chocolate and cannabis

Chong, Tommy- *n.* the cannabis legend from Cheech and Chong who supposedly defeated prostate cancer by using cannabis; also, *Tommy Chong* is famous for being incarcerated for selling Chong Bongs on the internet and for almost winning *Dancing With the Stars*

christen- *v.* to smoke or vape cannabis or cannabis concentrates though a new piece or implement; also, *christen* is to hotbox or otherwise smoke out a new vehicle, house or workplace to inaugurate one's presence and to clear out any negative energy like one might with a sage smudge to demons; *i.e. Why don't we christen our new hookah at the same time that we christen our new bed?*

Christmas trees- *n.pl. see tree*

chronic (chron, chrondo)- *n.* a gangsta colloquial term for exceptional cannabis; *chronic* was made famous by Dr. Dre and *The Chronic* album in 1992; also, the name was assumed by a breeding company for one of their strains, but is not the real *chronic* from the song

chunky- *adj.* having the quality of a cannabis bud structure that is thick and dense

Cindy 99- *n.* the sativa dominant cannabis heirloom legend *Cinderella 99* bred by Mr. Soul and The Brothers Grimm, a company that stopped producing seeds in 2004; *Cindy 99* is an unknown *Jack Herer* hybrid that has been used extensively in breeding programs worldwide; one of *Cindy 99's* claims to fame is that she is a sativa that flowers in seven to nine weeks instead of eleven to twenty weeks

cinnamon oil- *n.* a natural temporary pesticide that is safe for use on cannabis if diluted to no greater than a one percent solution when used independently; *cinnamon oil* is effective against sucking, mining and boring insects

Citral- *n.* the strain name given to several different varieties of the Chitral indica landrace; *for disambiguation, see Chitral, Citralah*

Citralah- *n.* an indica dominant cannabis strain bred by Soma's Sacred Seeds that is *Citral x Afghani Hawaiian; for disambiguation, see Chitral, Citral*

clambake- *v.* to hotbox a car, truck or motorhome; *see hotbox*

Clean Green Certification- *n.* an organic cultivation or processing certification for medical cannabis farms and medical cannabis processing facilities founded by Chris Van Hook, Esq. and associates; it is modeled after the USDA National Organic Program and has as strict or stricter requirements for cannabis crops; *i.e. It is hard for a dispensary owner to justify his medical validity if he fails to provide Clean Green Certified meds to his patients.*

clear the chamber- *phr.* the phrase used to describe the act of, or command the act of, drawing all the last of the smoke from the chamber of a pipe or bong in order to maximize one's intake and to prevent the etiquette violation of passing someone a bong with smoke still in the chamber (for that would be ghastly!)

clone- *n. see cutting, cultivar*

clone gel- *n.* a form of viscous commercial rooting hormone application that is typically not approved for use on food or cannabis crops, but is the most commonly used form of rooting method employed by cannabis cultivators; *i.e. I'd love to get a cutting of Chemdawg-4, but there is no guarantee that they didn't use a poisonous clone gel to root her.*

clone machine- *n.* a small aeroponic system suspended over a reservoir in which cannabis cuttings are inserted in small foam rings in order for a fine mist or spray of water to continuously saturate the cut end of the clone until it develops new roots; *i.e. One of the easiest, most productive and safest ways to clone cannabis is in a clone machine using distilled water and a small amount of organic B vitamin.*

clone-only- *adj.* a specific cannabis strain or cultivar that is only available as a clone and not in seed form; hoarding of *clone-only* strains has led to a loss of some of the best cannabis cultivars ever known

clone room (clone-room)- *n.* a veg room that is specifically controlled for the taking, rooting and hardening off of cuttings; often, the *clone room* is used for starting seeds as well; cultivators with the space and resources to manage more than two rooms often have a *clone room* due to the simple fact that seedlings or clones and rapidly growing plants in their vegetative state need drastically different environments from each other for optimum development

CO2- *abbrv. see carbon dioxide*

CO2 generator- *n.* a specialty propane burner that produces carbon dioxide for the purpose of enriching an indoor grow operation that operates in a closed system; typically, in places like areas of the UK, California and New York, *CO2 generators* are a waste of time, money, and hassle; these locations are not Canada or the arctic, and a fresh air exchange system will work as well or better than an operation running a *CO2 generator; see carbon dioxide, fresh air exchange*

CO2 oil- *n. see carbon dioxide, concentrate*

coaled- *adj.* having the characteristic of cannabis that has been coaled up; *see coal up*

coal up- *v.* the act of igniting a large bowl of cannabis completely on the first or second hit such that it remains burning like coal until it is completely ash

Coats vs. Dish Network- *n.* the groundbreaking legal case in which a paraplegic medical cannabis user sued Dish Network for wrongful termination after testing positive for cannabis and lost; citing the fact that the company has the right to have a no-tolerance drug policy in the workplace that Brandon Coats violated, the court dismissed the lawsuit; citing the fact that compassion trumps bullshit, we dismissed our Dish Network account and chose to abstain from financially supporting intolerant, hateful prohibitionists; *i.e. What kind of fucking*

*heartless corporation denies an employee who is a
motherfucking paraplegic his legally prescribed medicine? Had
he been on hydrocodone, a potentially lethal and highly
addictive narcotic, he would still have his job and there never
would have been a Coats vs. Dish Network for me to expose.*

cob- *n.* the traditional method of transporting and administering
Malawi; typically, a *cob* is approximately one ounce of cannabis
flowers on their stems wrapped in a banana leaf and tied together
to form a cob shape; *see Malawi*

coffee shop- *n.* an establishment in Amsterdam that sells
cannabis

coir- *n.* the natural fiber derived from the pith of coconut husks;
the only sustainable organic neutral growing medium currently
available; although coir is neutral, the raw product has a high
sodium content and must be thoroughly rinsed prior to use; also,
potassium, calcium, and magnesium tend to bind to coir making
them not immediately available to the roots, which must be taken
into consideration when applying amendments or nutrients

coir pellets- *n.pl.* small, compressed circles of coir wrapped in
netting that are reconstituted with water to be used for
germinating seeds or rooting cuttings; *for differentiation, see
peat pellets*

cola- *n.* the terminal flower on a cannabis plant; often, the *cola* is
the central-most flower, but not always; typically, the largest
buds on the plant; *cola* is spelled with a *c* not a *k*; the word is not
kola or *koala* (a koala bear is a marsupial, not a big bud)

collective- *n.* a term from California used for a dispensary due to
the original language in Prop 215; *see dispensary*

collie- *n.* an old school Jamaican word for excellent ganja, said
to be derived from the Indian deity Kali; an ankle-biting, cloying,
dirty and annoying breed of cur; *i.e. Laaaassssiee.... here, Lassie
girl, bring me my collie you greezy collie!*

colloidal silver- *n.* a solution of silver suspended in water that is used as a foliar spray in cannabis breeding to reverse a plant's gender in order to create feminized cannabis pollen for making *female-only* seeds

colloquial- *adj.* slang; I digress momentarily to ruminate on this simple definition of such an elegant expression, and to be inclusive of those, including my readership, who may have felt ostracized by the caliber of the verbiage used herein

Colorado cocktail- *n.* any cannabis from Colorado; the best kind of cocktail in the state

color tracer- *n.* the dye used by nutrient companies to make a fertilizer visible upon dilution in water; *color tracers* are yet another reason hydroponic cultivation is so atrocious: why does our beautiful cannabis have to be fed dyes?; *i.e. Anyone with any common sense can clearly see that cannabis should never be grown with anything that has a color tracer added to it.*

Columbian- *n.* a sativa dominant cannabis landrace originating in Columbia; ironically, much of the Mexican brick bud available in the United States during the late 1980s and 1990s was actually *Columbian* that was grown and processed in Mexico

comb- *n. see honey comb*

companion planting- *v.* sowing or growing varieties of ornamentals or other plants in conjunction with cannabis in order to utilize their natural pest prevention elements; common companion plants in the cannabis garden are pot marigolds (Calendula) and Pyrethrum daisies

compassion shelf- *n.* the ostentatious title given to the flowers a dispensary has designated for patients who need the medicine, but cannot afford top shelf, midgrade, or bottom shelf; most often, *compassion shelf* is actually a euphemism for *we don't*

give a shit about sick people, only profits… so we will make
ourselves look good by naming the shelf this, but will only stock
it with the worst of the worst of the worst flowers in the history of
humanity… flowers that have been blasted or are moldy or unfit
for human consumption for one reason or another… because
cannabis cash, not compassion, rules everything around me…;
—compassion-shelf *adj.* having the quality of compassion shelf;
for differentiation, see bottom shelf, house blend

compost- *n.* the decomposed organic material that is rich in
nutrients and microbiologicals and is commonly used in organic
cannabis cultivation; —*v.* to create *compost* by saving nutrient-
rich organic material like leaf mold, banana peels, egg shells,
shrimp and crab waste, alfalfa or other cover crops, and spent
cannabis parts (not stems, unless they have been through a
chipper-shredder), mixing them with a small amount of coir or
soil, and allowing them to decompose for weeks or months

compost tea- *n.* an oxygenated solution of steeped or brewed
compost or other amendments or organic fertilizers that is often
heavily employed in organic cannabis cultivation

concentrates- *n.pl.* concentrated forms of medical cannabis;
beach sand, bubble, budder*, butane honey oil*, cannoli, charas,
crumble*, crumz*, earwax*, finger hash, full extract cannabis
oil, full melt, glass*, hash, honey oil*, ISO hash*, kief, live
resin*, Milagro Oil, Obsidian Oil, oil*, Rick Simpson Oil*,
rosin, rosin tech, shatter*, and wax* are all names of various
concentrates using differing extraction methods; *typically made
with chemical solvents that can be toxic and potentially lethal or
explosive

cone- *n.* a large joint rolled in a conical shape; unless
manufactured or a house preroll, most *cones* contain a minimum
of two grams of cannabis, but are usually an eighth or more; the
shape your head feels after smoking certain strains like
Headband

Congolese (Congo)- *n.* an African sativa cannabis landrace from the Congolese region

connoisseur shelf- *n. see top shelf;* —*connoisseur-shelf adj.* having the quality of the connoisseur shelf

contact high- *n.* the name given to the state of being high through vicarious participation, osmosis, or diffusion; *i.e. That reporter claims she got a contact high from being in a hotboxed hotel room. What a fucking joke. Everyone knows it was the dab she did in the bathroom.*

contraband- *n.* yet another defining instance that clearly demonstrates the fact that The War on Drugs is founded, funded and fueled by racism; *contraband* was a slave, or slaves, who had escaped or *illegally* crossed Union lines; now, it's a term used for any illegal goods crossing boundary lines, or any goods that are imported or exported illegally; almost universally, *contraband* is used to describe shipments of cannabis, or illegal drugs, across state or country borders

conversion lamp- *n.* an HID lamp that will run on a ballast designed for a different type of lamp; *i.e. Many times, growers will run metal halide conversion lamps on high pressure sodium ballasts.*

cooperative (Co-op)- *n. see collective*

Corral, Valerie- *n. see WAMM*

cotton- *n.* an environmentally toxic and culturally detrimental crop grown with cancer-causing radioactive fertilizers and pesticides that has it roots firmly planted in the medium of racism; *cotton* could easily and safely be supplanted by the beneficial cannabis hemp crop

cottonmouth- *n.* the condition of extremely dry mouth and mucous membranes often associated with using cannabis, especially strains high in the terpene delta-3-carene; *see delta-3-carene*

cottonseed meal- *n.* due to the toxins used in cotton cultivation, *cottonseed meal* is not at all recommended for cannabis cultivation; *i.e. I try to avoid any amendment, like cottonseed meal, that was originally grown using dangerous pesticides and radioactive fertilizers.*

couchlock (couch lock, couch-lock)- *n.* the state of being so stoned from cannabis that one is unable to stand up from the couch; *couchlock* is a stereotypical stoner trait that is not applicable to the vast majority of cannabis strains or cannabis users; *see terpineol*

cough and you get off- *phr.* a cannabis smoking phrase popularized by Quentin Tarantino's 1997 film, *Jackie Brown,* that refers to the myth that one gets higher from cannabis smoke if it causes fits of coughing; the *cough and you get off* effect is not from the cannabis, but from a lack of oxygen to the brain; the truth is, top-quality cannabis should cause little or no coughing and the posers who sit there on YouTube coughing for minutes on end to their tiny *bomb shit* are douchy

Courtney, William- *n.* an innovative medical doctor located in Northern California who specializes in treating patients with cannabis, including with high CBD strains and fresh cannabis juice; the legend responsible for bringing the high CBD cannabis strain *ACDC* to the masses

cover crop- *n.* a specialized crop of plants grown specifically for their nutritional value to a subsequent crop; typically, *cover crops* are grown and tilled directly in the soil that will be used for the future crop, but can be grown, mowed and harvested for compost and other applications; occasionally, these crops are called green gold based on the fact that they are turned in the soil in a green state and are used as nutrient gold; great cannabis *cover crops* (for various reasons) include non-GMO soybeans, sunflowers, alfalfa, rye, and leguminous mixes with good nitrogen fixing ability

Crazy Eighths- *n.* a passive gang of confused cannabis smokers; also, *Crazy Eighths* is a cannabis party game where a group of eight, sixteen, or thirty-two people place two eighths each on the playing table, one in the center *pot*, and one directly in front of them like a hand of cards; then, an objective or blind third party plays Bob Marley's song *Kaya* while the group members rotate around the table in the spirit of musical chairs; when the music stops, everyone sits down to the pile in front of them and begins consuming the eighth in a pipe, vaporizer, or bong (no papers or blunts allowed); the first person to finish smoking or vaping the entire eighth with panache, as judged by the members of the gathering, gets the center *pot*; style and overall smoke or vapor consumed is taken into consideration by the crowd when being judged (to avoid contestants burnin' without inhalin' and to give props to smoke blowing masters or other inventive tokers)

creamy smoke- *n.* any cannabis smoke that is thick or expansive, especially one that produces a milky white cloud upon exhale; *see smoke expansion;* *—creamy adj.* having the characteristics of *creamy smoke*

creeper- *n.* a strain that has a delayed onset of effects after inhalation; *—adj.* having the characteristic of cannabis that lurks for awhile and then sneaks up on you like a mindfucking stalker; *—creep v.* to have the effects of cannabis inhalation delayed, usually with some sensation of suspense; *i.e. Watch out for that creeper Trainwreck, because it can be creepy when it creeps up on you like a creeper.*

crispy- *adj.* having the quality or characteristic of old, dried-out cannabis or of cannabis leaves that have been scorched by excessive nutrients or horticultural lighting; also, *crispy* is often used to describe one or one's state of being after consuming cannabis; *i.e. She blew cannabis vape hits into her cat's face until he was a crispy critter.*

crop dusting- *v.* walking around a room or through the crowd of a gathering while taking continuous hits from a bong, pipe or joint along the way; *i.e. The only way I can handle a large party is by crop dusting the whole time.*

cross- *n. see hybrid;* —*v.* to breed two or more cannabis strains together

crossfade- *v.* to consume cannabis and alcohol simultaneously; to tempt fate; to taint something beautiful with a poison; *see stammered*

cross joint- *n.* a joint rolled into the shape of a cross; *i.e. Actor Seth Rogen can roll a mean cross joint.*

cross pollinate- *v. see cross*

crumb (crumbs)- *n. see crumble*

crumble- *n.* a specific type of solvent-extracted cannabis concentrate so named for the crumbly texture of the final product; typically, *crumble* is one of the highest quality solvent-extracted concentrates that has not been made into an absolute; —*to crumble v.* what exposing the truth about cannabis will do to the foundation of the wall of prohibition

crumz (crums)- *n.* a slightly idiotic colloquialism for cannabis crumble

crutch- *n.* a small fold of card stock paper rolled into the mouth end of a joint or cone as a make-shift filter; what prohibitionists use to support their lies and hydrocodone-laden thighs

crystals- *n.pl.* shiny, diamond-like glandular trichomes on mature cannabis; the shimmering effect is the result of light passing through active glands still producing resin; appropriately harvested cannabis will look "crystally" [sic] (to the entire stoner population); overripe cannabis looks dusty, not crystalline; *i.e. Remember at harvest time, if your crystals are shinin' like yellow* *diamonds, you're climbin'... if they're brown like the ground, you're put down.*

cubes- *n.pl.* the cuboidal rockwool chunks of various sizes, including small pea-sized squares and big boss-sized bricks, used for hydroponic cultivation; *see rockwool*

cull- *v.* to thin or kill select plants for specific reasons; often, a cannabis gardener will *cull* any weak or diseased seedlings and replant if necessary to have the most vigorous and healthy garden possible; *cull* is not to be confused with what Trump plans to do to the US population if he's elected tyrant...er...president

cultivar- *n.* a cannabis strain that has been produced in cultivation through selective breeding for its specific traits; typically, a cultivar is passed along in the form of a cutting or clone; often, cultivars are patented or trademarked agricultural varieties of certain food crops, and this soon may apply to cannabis as well; *see cutting*

Culture- *n.* a cannabis magazine with regional editions that is focused more on the culture of cannabis and cannabis users rather than on growing and politics like their contemporary, *High Times; i.e. Hey, there's a copy of High Times, wanna pick it up? 'Nah, let's get a copy of Culture... I think it's more apropos.'*

cup winner- *n.* a cannabis strain, concentrate or product that has earned at least one of the major cannabis cup awards; *i.e. My Butterfly strain is sure to be a cup winner... if I cared enough to play those games. Like a wise man once said, "The best cannabis in the world is never the cup winner, because the people who grow the world's greatest strains don't give a flyin' fuck about a popularity contest. After all, they're too busy growing and smoking that shit to care what the cool kids think of them."*

cure- *v.* to dry and age cannabis flowers in a controlled environment with the proper temperature and humidity until the time at which the chlorophyll has degraded and the terpenes are their most vibrant; quality cannabis is dried for about two weeks, then aged or *cured* for another two to twenty-five weeks, depending on the strain, in order to remove the vegetal flavor and allow the terpenes to shine; proper *curing* does not readily decarboxylate cannabis from THCa to THC to CBN, whereas improper *curing* can turn the medicine harsh or into a higher CBN flower; —*n.* what cannabis is to society's decay; *cure* is not to be confused with *Curare*, which is the poison from the plant Strychnos *toxifera* used to tip arrows for hunting; *Curare* causes paralysis and death if the poisoned person's respiratory system is not maintained artificially; one should *cure* cannabis, not *Curare* it

cured- *adj.* having the quality of dried and aged cannabis flowers; what many people are after using medical cannabis; *see cure*

cutting- *n.* a small, tender branch of cannabis that has been cut off a donor or mother plant and allowed to root on its own; a form of vegetative or asexual propagation; beware of clone gels or rooting compounds for cannabis: if the label says, "Not for use on food crops," it is not intended for use on cannabis; *for differentiation, see cultivar*

cutting the grass (mowing the lawn)- *phr.* a colloquialism for smoking or otherwise consuming cannabis; *i.e. It's so fun to answer the what are you doing this weekend question with a simple statement that I'm going to be cutting the grass.*

CVault- *n. see canister*

cystolithic trichomes- *n.pl. see trichome*

cytokinins- *n.pl.* a group of plant hormones that promote cell division in plant roots and new-growth tips or shoots; synthetic and commercial cannabis fertilizers and nutrients are often supplemented with *cytokinins* to stimulate root development and growth

D- *abbrv.* a dab

dab- *v.* to *dab*; —*n.* a concentrate placed on top of a bowl of flowers, a red-hot nail or other device for immediate vaporization and inhalation; causes instantaneous and extreme euphoria; a *dab* can be beneficial for those with a high tolerance, but is not at all recommended for novices; often, *dabs* are extracted using solvents that can never be removed no matter how well they are purged, and therefore are not usually recommended for use by anyone; the term gets its name from the original act of taking a little *dab* of hash and putting it on a bowl of flowers as a topper; *i.e. Since a person can rarely tell if a dab is clean, a general rule of thumb is: "A little dab'll doom ya.";* see purge, topper

dabable- *adj.* having the characteristic of a concentrate that is able to be dabbed instead of combusted

dabbabble- *v.* to dabble or casually participate in dabbing, usually only at a party; *dabbabble* is like the dabber version of what one may call social cigarette smoking; also, *dabbabble* is to babble on and on after taking a dab

dabber- *n.* one who dabs; one who is already dead, just doesn't know it yet; the exception is a *dabber* who truly only uses Clean Green solvent-less organic concentrates like rosin or bubble; *i.e. Because of the exploding concentrate labs, the public perception of dabbers is often that they are the trashiest of trashy people like how piss-beer, generic vodka, or malt-liquor drinkers are perceived in mainstream culture.;* also, a *dabber* is another word for a dab tool, as in: a *dabber* is a tool

dabhead (dab head, dhead, Dhead)- *n.* derogatory for one who dabs; *i.e. There are far too many Dheads at the cups these days for them to be worth attending at all anymore.*

dab rig (dab-rig, rig)- *n.* the smoking or vaping apparatus used to dab waxes and other (typically solvent-extracted) cannabis concentrates; —*v.* to sabotage a dabber's rig

dab tool- *n.* the metal, glass, ceramic, or wood tool used to take a cannabis concentrate from its dish and place it on the nail of a dab rig

dagga- *n.* a South African word for cannabis that is often used colloquially throughout the rest of the world

damping off (damping-off)- *n.* a general term for any number of soil or medium-borne pathogens, like Pythium, that weaken, consume, or otherwise compromise the integrity of seeds or seedlings; *damping off* is most common in overly damp, wet or acidic soils or mixes… which is one of many reasons that peat-based mediums are less ideal for cannabis cultivation than, say, an amendment-rich, light and loamy soil that has been mechanically aerated with a soil conditioner like pumice stone

dance with Mary Jane- *phr.* to smoke cannabis; adds new meaning to Tom Petty's song and video… so are we to believe that cannabis is a dead Kim Basinger?

dank- *n.* strong smelling cannabis that often has musty, musky or skunky overtones; —*adj.* expressing the quality of strong smelling cannabis

David, Jayden- *n.* a brave young child from California with Dravet syndrome who has had his life saved by the use of high CBD and high THC medical cannabis extracts and who has become the face of defeating Dravet with cannabis

dazed- *adj.* a term for having the characteristics of being stoned and out of it

Dazed and Confused- *n.* an iconic, coming-of-age stoner film released in 1993

dealer- *n.* one who illegally sells cannabis and other drugs; what many dispensary owners actually are, despite the documents on the wall

DeAngelo, Steve- *n. see Harborside*

decarboxylate- *v.* to remove a carboxyl group from a chemical compound; in cannabis, this means to convert THCa to THC in order to activate it for the psychoactive effect (or CBDa to CBD, etc.); smoking or vaping *decarboxylates* cannabis immediately upon inhalation, however edible cannabis must be *decarboxylated* prior to ingestion; *see stoned rabbits*

decriminalization- *n.* the act of removing the criminal or punitive aspect of some outlawed substance, action or concept; when it comes to cannabis reform, one must be clear on the difference between actual *decriminalization* and *decriminalization* as proposed by prohibitionists; *decriminalization,* in its truest sense, is a complete removal of all criminality from cannabis, making it entirely legal for any and all to use as if it were a tomato or any other food crop; prohibitionists' definition of *decriminalization* simply means keeping cannabis illegal entirely, but reducing the penalties, and is bullshit; *for differentiation, see legalization*

deep water (deep water aquaculture)- *n. see aquaculture*

deliveries (delivery services)- *n.pl.* (legal, medical) cannabis dispensaries or services that operate without a store front or functional brick-and-mortar establishment; ostensibly, many *deliveries* are simply drug dealers open to advertise to the public; in large cities of prohibition states like New York, *delivery services* often take the form of beautiful model couriers in tight, slutty attire delivering top-shelf buds to your door such that your little friend gets high before you can even smoke that shit; *for differentiation, see brick-and-mortar*

delta-3-carene- *n.* a common terpene found in cannabis that has a woody aroma; as it is one of the primary medical constituents of cedar, *delta-3-carene* has undergone numerous scientific studies that have determined its efficacy in drying out mucous membranes; *delta-3-carene* is partially responsible for cottonmouth and is further proof that cannabis is indeed an invaluable medicine; *see cottonmouth*

delta 9 (Δ9)- *n. see tetrahydrocannabinol*

deodorizers- *n.pl.* the group of masking agents or odor minimizing chemicals used to prevent the spread of cannabis odors from a grow op, or to disguise the presence of cannabis smoke; *deodorizers* range from intermittent perfume sprayers and deodorizing agent aerosolizers to scented gels and beads and the omnipresent and stereotypical Nag Champa incense

depletion (nutrient depletion)- *n. see nutrient deficiency*

deuce- *n. see dub*

deuce deuce- *n.* a heavy dub; two grams of cannabis; a gun; *i.e. Put the deuce deuce down, dumbshit. I gotta deuce deuce over here you can have that is so much better for humanity and society.*

devil weed (devilweed, Devil's Weed, Devil's Lettuce)- *n.* a shameful, insulting, scaremongering colloquialism for cannabis; not to be confused with the *hop*, which is used to flavor your sacred beer

dewax- *v.* to remove the fats, lipids or plant waxes from a cannabis concentrate through the application of dry ice or the use of a specialized filter or secondary solvent; *for differentiation, see absolute, winterization*

Dhead- *abbrv. see dabhead*

diatomaceous earth (DTE)- *n.* a fine, porous and powdery sedimentary deposit formed from the fossil remains of diatoms that is used in cannabis cultivation as an all-natural pesticide for crawling and wiggling insects and as a soil conditioner that adds trace amounts of plant-available silica to the medium over time

dietary cannabis- *n.* any cannabis that has not been decarboxylated and that is intended for human nutritional consumption, including but not limited to cannabis seed oil, cannabis seed, cannabis seed cake, cannabis protein powder, fresh cannabis flowers, fresh cannabis leaf, cannabis sap, or cannabis juice

diffuser- *n.* a specific type of percolator or bong with multiple chambers

digital ballast (electronic ballast)- *n. see ballast*

dime (dime bag)- *n.* a small bag of cannabis containing ten dollars worth of flowers; *for disambiguation, see drop a dime*

Dinafem- *n.* an intriguing breeding company that gets its fame for being possibly the most well-known Spanish cannabis breeders

dirtweed (dirt weed, dirt bud, dirt)- *n. see Mexican brick bud*

dish- *n.* the container used for transporting or storing cannabis concentrates

dispensary- *n.* a medical cannabis pharmacy; a legal establishment for administering medical cannabis; for some *dispensaries*, it's a tax-free way to make millions; since most banks won't take cannabis income, who's to say how much in taxes *dispensaries* actually have to pay

dissolvable tabs- *n.pl. see tabs*

ditch weed (ditchweed)- *n.* a colloquial term for Midwestern United States landrace cannabis hemp; due to the nature of genetics and breeding, most ditchweed is low in cannabinoids, however there are documented cases of ditchweed testing over twenty percent THC in many samples and up to seventeen percent CBD in others; gutter money

djamba- *n.* a West African word for cannabis used colloquially worldwide

doctor's rec. (doctor's recommendation)- *n. see verification*

doja- *n.* a colloquialism for cannabis, especially purple cannabis flowers

dolomite lime- *n. see lime*

dome- *n.* the curved and rounded apparatus fixed over a hot nail on a dab rig to encourage the vapor to find its home down the tube and in the lungs of the dabber

domeless nail- *n.* this one is so obvious even a dabhead could figure it out; *see dome, nail*

dominant- *adj.* heavily favoring one side; in regards to cannabis hybrids, strains are either *sativa dominant, ruderalis dominant,* or *indica dominant*; to all the supposed breeders and pollen slingers out there, a reminder: the word is *dominant*, not *dominate*

donation- *n.* due to the ridiculousness of law, the term applied to all money or goods exchanged within the medical cannabis system in some legal states; a *donation* can simply be the money one pays to a dispensary, prior to taxes (ironically), for a quantity of medical cannabis or medical cannabis products; or, it can be the actual cannabis a provider gives to the dispensary in exchange for a return *donation* of tax-free cash

donkey dick (donkey)- *n.* a truly *ass*inine colloquialism for giant cannabis flowers with a purple hue

donor- *n. see mother*

doobage- *n. see doobie*

Doobian Queen (Doobian Princess)- *n.* a gorgeous and sensual woman, typically one of color, who consumes a great quantity of cannabis

doobie- *n.* a joint; occasionally, *doobie* is used in the plural form *doobage* to mean cannabis in general, or a quantity of cannabis joints or flowers; *doobie* was popularized by the southern rockers of the US

doobieous- *adj.* of or relating to authentic, albeit cynical and sardonic, cannabis terms and definitions of questionable moral character

doobie snacks- *n.pl.* colloquial for cannabis, specifically multiple cannabis joints; also, *doobie snacks* can refer to munchies or food that is consumed after cannabis ingestion; the term gets its provenance from the fact that Scooby and Shaggy seem to be raging fucking potheads always eating Scooby Snacks; *see munchies*

dope- *n.* a derogatory euphemism for cannabis; due to the typical connotation of *dope* being heroin, the word is used by prohibitionists to inflame and confuse the ignorant masses; if prohibitionists can get uneducated people to believe that cannabis is as bad as heroin, and that only black and Mexican people use it, then surely the whites will be scared enough to keep buying the booze; —*adj.* an expression of good quality, based on cannabis users adopting the term to diffuse its negative power, like the homosexual community did with the word *queer*; *i.e. That City Blues tarantula was fuckin' dope!*

**double *0* powder *(00 powder, 00* Moroccan, *00)-* *n.* a type of kief that gets its name from the size of the silk screen used to sift or separate the glandular trichomes from the vegetal cannabis material; other grades of kief similar to *00* are also named after the size of silk screen, for example, *0* powder

Draconian laws- *n.pl.* the description given by cannabis reformers to the archaic and sadistic prohibition laws still burdening our worldwide health and economy; the juxtaposition originates from the extreme rigor and cruelty imparted to law by the Athenian statesman, Draco, under whom moderate offenses held severe punishments, and its similarities to The War on Drugs

drag- *n.* an inhalation of cannabis smoke, typically from a joint; —*take a drag v.* to inhale a *drag* of cannabis smoke from a joint; *i.e. Take di drag offa dis collie, mon.;* for the record, bright neon or multicolored, floral-print rolling papers are not considered to be cannabis *drag*

drama- *n. see weed people*

draw- *v.* to pull smoke or vapor through a pipe, bong, joint or other smoking or vaping apparatus; to *draw* is not to be confused with *to puff*, as it is longer and more prolonged than the short puff; *for differentiation, see hit, drag, puff*

'dro- *abbrv.* hydro; used in direct reference to hydroponic grown cannabis; *i.e. My bro with the 'fro got some ho he know to grow him some mean 'dro, yo.; see hydro, hydroponic*

drop a dime- *v.* to call the police on someone for their cannabis or other drug use; *drop a dime* has become archaic due to the extinction of pay telephones… nowadays it's probably called something like *flick an EM button* or some shit

drought- *n.* the state of being without cannabis, or in an area without available cannabis; *i.e. Man, it sucks balls when were in such a drought… I'm getting real thirsty for some bud right about now.;* a cannabis *drought* is not to be confused with a meteorological drought… that kind of drought gets blamed on cannabis users, but give me a break… do you really think that the average of three gallons of water per large outdoor cannabis plant every two or three days is really as detrimental as all the golf courses, the department store sprinklers constantly gushing water from broken pipes, the ridiculous meat-market STD exchange locations known as water parks, the rich whiteys filling their million-dollar pools, or the horse ranchers who waste every drop of ten gallons of water per horse every day on nothing more than a glorified, smelly stuffed fucking animal (I mean, really, we can't even eat horses, so why raise them? Oh... now I know... your wife is unsatisfied and too embarrassed to buy a sybian)

drug dealer- *n. see dealer*

drug strain- *n.* any strain, variety, cultivar or landrace of cannabis that is produced for its cannabinoid content rather than for its textile or fiber content; interestingly, as cannabis has become more widely legalized, and hemp has again become one of the world's preeminent crops, agricultural scientists are finding that certain *drug strains* are actually better textile strains than the current best of the best available to hemp farmers; *for differentiation, see textile strain*

drug testing- *n.* the archaic and barbaric practice of invading a future or current employee's private life with emotional rape in order to protect the company heads from the embarrassment of a drug-addled and productive workforce; after all, the companies are already far too marred by their infidelities and murderous transgressions to ever allow themselves to get caught up in a cannabis scandal; *see Coats vs. Dish Network*

dry- *v.* to slowly remove the moisture content from cannabis flowers over time through the use of evaporation; —*adj.* the state or condition of lacking moisture, typically used to describe cannabis flowers that have been dried or cured past the proper point; also, a term used to describe an area without available cannabis or the condition of being without cannabis; *i.e. I cannot wait to dry my new harvest, because it's been dry as shit around town. I sure as fuck won't have to worry about one bud of it gettin' too dry... I tell you what!*

dry ice extraction- *n.* a style of making kief that uses dry ice to readily separate the glandular trichomes from the cannabis plant material due to the subfreezing temperatures

drying rack- *n.* a netted or screened apparatus in which fresh-cut cannabis flowers are laid or hung in order to dry prior to curing; a *drying rack* is not to be confused with the drunk tank, which is where slobs dry out

dry sieve (dry sift)- *n. see kief, sift*

DTE- *abbrv. see diatomaceous earth*

dual arc- *n.* a type of HID lamp that contains both metal halide and high pressure sodium arcs

dual extraction method- *n. see absolute, winterization, dewax*

dub- *n.* a quantity of cannabis for sale equal to twenty dollars worth; usually, a *dub* is one gram of top-shelf cannabis flower

dub sack- *n.* a dub in a bag; *see dub*

Ducksfoot (Duck's Foot)- *n.* a sativa dominant cannabis heirloom strain out of Australia that was popularized by Wally Duck; *Ducksfoot* stands out from the crowd because she has leaves with fused leaflets, ultimately presenting with a palmately lobed leaf structure that looks like the foot of a duck

dug out (dug out pipe)- *n.* a specific type of one-hitter that is flat in shape and often made of wood or metal

dust- *adj.* having the quality of a bowl that is ashy or empty; *i.e. This one's dust, yo… y'all want me to pack another bowl of Certified 20?*

dutchie- *n.* a joint; occasionally, *dutchie* is used colloquial for a blunt rolled in a Dutch Masters' wrapper; this word was popularized in the song *Pass the Dutchie* by Musical Youth in 1982; the song is virtually a how-to on smoking a joint or blunt in a group: take two hits, then "pass the *dutchie* on the left-hand side…"

66

Eagle 20- *n. see pesticides*

Earl- *n.* a colloquial term for oil or concentrates used in the same spirit as *Mary Jane* for cannabis flowers; *i.e. My clean, green uncle Earl, who is one straight G, showed up this mornin' to make my day fuckin' great!*

Earleywine, Mitch- *n.* a professor of psychology for the State University of New York at Albany who is on the frontlines in promoting the benefits of cannabis and is known for discrediting so-called scientific psychological studies that vilify cannabis

earwax- *n. see wax*

eating a sandwich- *phr.* a euphemism used to mean smoking or consuming cannabis, specifically smoking a joint, that was popularized by the lit television series *How I Met Your Mother*

ebb and flow (ebb 'n' flow, flood and drain)- *n.* a type of hydroponic cannabis cultivation where a nutrient solution fills a tray of cannabis plants in containers or rockwool and then is drained away immediately after the medium has wicked up the necessary volume of fluid; this process is repeated periodically throughout the day with the frequency of flooding dependent upon the rate of absorption and evaporation

EC- *abbrv. see electrical conductivity*

edible- *n. see medible*

eighth- *n.* one-eighth of an ounce; the designation given to an amount equal to three and one-half grams of cannabis; in this current culture, it bears repeating: there are three and one-half grams in an *eighth*, not four grams, no matter what some dipshit dispensaries claim; *i.e. Just like a half-way crook, there ain't no such thing as a four-gram eighth!*

Eighth Crazy Nights- *n.* the eight nights of Hanukkah where the faithful smoke or vape one eighth of cannabis each evening in honor of the sacred kaneh bosom

electrical conductivity (EC)- *n.* the amount of electricity that can pass through a length of something; in terms of cannabis cultivation, testing *electrical conductivity* is one of the ways to determine the salt concentration of a hydroponic nutrient solution

Emerald Triangle, The- *n.* the storied location of the world's greatest outdoor cannabis cultivation, or so they keep repeatedly reminding us, comprised of Humboldt, Mendocino and Trinity Counties in California; supposedly, *The Emerald Triangle* is responsible for producing over seventy percent of all cannabis in the US; just because you can mass produce cannabis does not make your product the best... just look at Walmart; rarely, *The Emerald Triangle* refers to the common cannabis producing areas of Florida: Miami, Jacksonville, and Tampa

Emery, Marc- *n.* the Prince of Pot; a Canadian cannabis hero who is known for creating *Cannabis Culture Magazine* and *Pot TV*, and for being the only person who was incarcerated (2009-2014) in the US for selling cannabis seeds in Canada and through mail-order

endogenous cannabinoid- *n. see cannabinoid; anandamide*

enhancement smoker- *n.* supposedly, this is the type of stoner who tries to convince everyone else that all things are better with cannabis; frankly, anyone who has ever consumed cannabis knows that everything is in fact better with cannabis and therefore is a de facto *enhancement smoker*

entourage effect- *n.* the term given to the medical amplification that occurs in whole-plant medical cannabis use as opposed to single extractive medicine use; science has shown that terpenes and cannabinoids work together synergistically to create a greater medical benefit than any individually isolated cannabinoid or terpene; the results of studies on the *entourage* *effect* are primary evidence in the argument for whole-plant cannabis medicine; the *entourage effect* is not to be confused with the nausea experienced from watching the hit show

environmental controller- *n.* a device employed in the indoor garden that regulates the on and off schedule of the equipment used in the growing of cannabis, like horticultural lighting and fans

enzymes- *n.pl.* a general term for the group of proteins that act as a catalyst for complex reactions in plant growth; specifically, *enzymes* are useful in cannabis cultivation as a natural means to break down old and dead or damaged root tissue in the soil to make room for new roots

e-pen (ePen)- *n.* a vape pen designed specifically for concentrates; due to the potential of explosion, use of these products is not recommended

Epsom salt- *n. see magnesium sulfate*

eradication units- *n.pl.* intolerant, violent, and often brutal groups of police officers charged with perpetuating the holocaust against cannabis users; in legal states, *eradication units* are most often found in banned counties, or are rogue militia groups operating illegally within cannabis-friendly counties or cities; these *eradication units* have been caught burning the property of legal cannabis users, tearing out cannabis gardens in the cover of dark and without hiding behind their badge, and setting up legitimate cannabis business owners and then providing false testimony against them in court; in prohibition states, *eradication units* frequently break down people's doors, shoot their dogs to death in front of their toddlers, and arrest them all because they stumbled upon wet tea leaves and a receipt for generalized fertilizers in their trash can; *i.e. I wonder when the karma train is going to run over the members of eradication units.*

errl- *n.* colloquial for oil, as if saying the word properly is too much effort or far too intellectually challenging for the dabber

escapism- *n.* the act of escaping from reality; in regards to cannabis, *escapism* is one of the numerous fallacious side effects of cannabis consuption; in fact, cannabis users often become more present, fully aware of all the universal mechanics occurring at every millisecond, so completely living in the sensation of the now moment that they are often accused of being in outer space; *i.e. When life feels this fucking great all the time, escapism becomes more boring than reality.*

ether- *n.* diethyl ether, (C2H5)2; a highly volatile colorless liquid hallucinogen that was formerly used in general anesthesia and for early cannabis extraction; can cause etheromania, a temporary addictive state sometimes known as Bieber Fever, and is not to be confused with a sexually transmitted disease

eucalyptol- *n.* a common terpene found in cannabis that has a spicy mint aroma; as it is one of the primary medical constituents of eucalyptus and rosemary, *eucalyptol* has undergone numerous scientific studies that have determined its efficacy in its ability to increase circulation and blood flow; *eucalyptol* is further proof that cannabis is indeed an invaluable medicine

euphoria- *n.* a state or feeling of intense, extreme excitement and happiness; *euphoria* is the typical result of consuming cannabis, if one can allow oneself to be happy

exit bag- *n.* a specific type of child-resistant bag employed by cannabis stores in Colorado; ridiculous piece of mind for paranoid prohibitionists... if they truly cared about children and public safety and not just their anti-cannabis platform, they would make sure all alcohol and bleach and cigarettes and foxgloves and coffee and plastic bags and pharmaceuticals... were only allowed out of the door of a store if they are sealed in a child-resistant *exit bag*... but, it seems that prohibitionists aren't actually concerned with kids or public wellbeing; *see Adult Use of Marijuana Act, Blue Ribbon Commission, reformer*

Exodus- n. see Cheese

expando weed- *n.* any cannabis flowers that produce creamy smoke or that cause smoke expansion; *see smoke expansion*

expand your mind- *phr.* the evidence used by one's friends to persuade one who is intellectual or creative by nature into using cannabis for the first time; *i.e. C'mon, it's totally safe and it can expand your mind.*; in reality, one of the world's greatest examples of coincidence is that recent scientific studies have shown cannabis consumption to increase and expand the number and frequency of neural connections throughout the cerebral cortex while occasionally decreasing the mass size of the grey matter

expansion- *n. see smoke expansion*

extract- *n.* duh; *see concentrates;* —*v.* the process of removing the resin or the glandular trichome heads from cannabis material by force, through the application of cold or heat, or with some sort of solvent; —*n.* the result of such action

extract artist- *n.* one who specializes in making top quality cannabis extracts like rosin, solvent-less bubble, or solvent-extracted concentrates; *i.e. Being a real artist, one who paints, writes prose, satire and poetry, and makes artisan soap, it is difficult for me to stomach most instances of people referring to themselves as extract artists. It's kinda like calling someone who cooks meth an artist simply because he has enough of a chemical background or understanding to produce a quality product from a recipe he read online.; for differentiation, see hashmaker*

extraction- *n. see extract*

extractor- *n.* a specialty device or machine designed to complete the process of or assist in the completion of extracting cannabinoids, terpenes, or glandular trichomes from cannabis; there are numerous types of *extractors*, including oil presses, tumblers, and bubble machines; *see Queen Bee Extractor, tumbler, oil press, bubble machine*

F1- *abbrv.* filial generation one; the offspring resulting from the original cross of two parents; *i.e. When it comes to breeding, look at it like this: you are the F1 of your momma and the motherfucking mailman.*

faded- *adj.* having the quality of being so stoned that one becomes slightly sleepy and dimming

fail-tech- *n.* absolutely every single concentrate made with any solvent other than water, CO2, or glycerin

Fairbanks, Matt- *n.* the DEA agent who testified under oath that Utah should not legalize medical cannabis because it will cause all the feral rabbits to get stoned; *Fairbanks* swore that his information is based on science yet everyone knows about decarboxylation; he should be cited and jailed ex post facto for perjury; *see stoned rabbits, decarboxylation*

fake plastic trees- *n.pl.* cannabis flowers grown with hydroponic nutrients or synthetic all-purpose fertilizers; *see pretty trash*

farmacies- *n.pl.* oftentimes disreputable, though technically legal, cannabis dispensaries; *i.e. I heard they finally closed those ghetto farmacies out in the country.*

fatty- *n. see phatty*

feather meal- *n.* a natural fertilizer or amendment made from the ground feathers left over from commercial chicken and turkey slaughtering facilities; *feather meal* is high in slow-release nitrogen, which makes it appealing for long-season outdoor cannabis cultivation; but, *feather meal* is not recommended for use on cannabis due to the risk of contamination

feces-free- *adj.* having the quality of cannabis cultivation that does not use any animal feces in order to minimize the risk of possible contaminants in the finished flowers; *feces-free* cultivation refrains from using bat guano, manure, chicken shit or any other form of animal defecation including human, but typically allows for the use of worm castings

FECO (feco, fec)- *acronym see full extract cannabis oil*

FECOff (fecoff)- *v.* to use FECO; *i.e. Hey Ben Carson, why don't you go FECOff, so you actually know what you're talking about instead of regurgitating hate and ignorance in the form of staunch cannabis prohibition. You have a moral and legal obligation as a doctor to prevent harm, not cause suffering... it's called the Hippocratic Oath, not the Hypocritical Oath.*

feed- *v.* to give cannabis plants nourishment

feeling your hair growing (hearing your hair grow)- *phr.* the description used by many first time or novice cannabis users who get astronomically high, so high that almost all will announce in astonishment: "I think I can feel my hair growing!"

feminized (fem)- *adj.* having the quality or characteristic of being artificially made to be female (so, maybe it should be added to the community list: LGBT*F*); in the breeding business, this is a term used to describe cannabis seeds that should produce only female plants; the industrial process to feminize cannabis is unnatural, and occasionally uses systemic toxins that are unsafe; in truth, *feminized* means female or hermaphroditic, and all *feminized* seed plants need to be subjected to the least amount of stress possible; coddle your *fem* plants, and monitor them well for any signs of big ol' balls or ninja hermies

feminized pollen- *n.* the result of using colloidal silver, gibberellins, or other external stressors to reverse the gender of a female cannabis plant and force her to create male flowers that release pollen; this *feminized pollen* carries the genetic material of the female, and can be used to pollinate other females and create offspring that lack any male genetic potential; *feminized pollen* creates offspring that are either female or hermaphroditic; many people in the cannabis community and breeding business consider *feminized pollen* to be unnatural, however the hermaphroditic tendencies of cannabis exist independently from the external stress used to initiate or trigger its presence… therefore, *feminized pollen* isn't unnatural *per se*, but rather the methods often employed by commercial breeders to create said pollen are arguably unnatural

ferret- *v.* to water and fertilize at the same time; little did you know that the hydroponic weasels were so self-aware

fiber strain- *n. see textile strain*

filial generation one- *n. see F1*

finger hash- *n. see hashish*

finishing solution- *n. see flushing solution*

fire (fyah)- *n.* a colloquialism for potent, aromatic or harsh cannabis flowers that is at the center of a heated debate: is the word *fire or fyah?*; *i.e. I heard that girl bitch about how many weed people are so stupid that they can't even say the word fire correctly.; —adj.* having the characteristic of cannabis that is so hot it's smokin'

fire it up- *phr.* to light up some cannabis

fix- *n.* the satisfaction of receiving the holy sacrament of cannabis after an extended period of fasting or Lenten reconciliation like one experiences in times of drought or employment; *i.e. Man, I been at work all day and I need a fix right now.*

flat stems- *n.pl.* a specific cannabis trait found in some *Pakistani* landrace strains and their hybrids; unlike the normal cylindrical shape, cannabis with *flat stems* has stems that are shaped more like a dog bone, with a flat middle and slightly convex bulbous ends on both sides

flavorbomb- *v.* to drop a dab on a nail that has been heated to a lower temperature in order to only vaporize the terpenes; the dabber's attempt to recapture the beautiful flavors and aromas of the original cannabis flower from the extract by using a lower temperature and concentrating really hard on believing that it possibly tastes anywhere near as good as cannabis flowers; *i.e. Flavorbombing concentrates seems like a waste of money when the flowers taste way better anyway. If you need to get higher, smoke or vape more flowers. And, don't give me that bullshit that it is safer for the lungs to only take a dab or two than it is to vape an oven or two. I call BULLSHIT on that dumb-ass logic.; see purge*

floatin'- *adj. see soarin'*

flood and drain- *n. see ebb and flow*

flower- *n.* the most usable part of a cannabis plant; the highest concentration of active cannabinoids occurs in a perfectly ripe cannabis *flower*; cannabis *flowers* are harvested, dried and cured before being administered; *i.e. It is awesome that the largest counterculture group in the world is founded on a flower...we're basically all just a bunch of fuckin' flower-power hippies, aren't we?;* —*v.* to cause a cannabis plant to produce blossoms, buds and flowers; —*flowering adj.* having the characteristic of a cannabis plant that is in bloom or in flower

flower bar- *n.* the display counter in a dispensary specifically for dried flowers, not concentrates, medibles, topicals, seeds, or cuttings; a *flower bar* is not to be confused with a hippie granola bar

flower room- *n.* the indoor room that is specifically designated for flowering cannabis plants under a twelve-twelve light cycle; *for differentiation, see mother room, veg room, clone room*

flower structure (bud structure)- *n.* the physical expression of structural traits in the cannabis flowers or buds of a specific strain or phenotype of a strain; *flower structure* in cannabis varies greatly depending on genetic composition and environmental factors like light intensity, nutrient level, and temperature; flowers can represent in a number of ways, from long, running colas completely filled in with hundreds of smaller flowers, to large, chunky, golf-ball-shaped flower clusters attached to spindly stems with long internode length; *i.e. I dig the flower structure of Cracker Jack, even though it isn't super chunky.*

fluorescent lighting (fluorescents)- *n.* possibly the least expensive and least effective form of horticultural lighting; *fluorescent lighting* comes in many sizes and intensities, including T-12, T-8, T-5, HO, and VHO, and are virtually a waste of money for most cannabis cultivators; the light intensity versus heat output versus electricity usage of *fluorescents* makes them impractical for anyone attempting to seriously cultivate cannabis; *i.e. Thanks to advancements in technology, LED lighting is a far greater value than fluorescents.*

flushing (flush)- *v.* feeding plants that have finished flowering a solution of pure water, or a salt-leeching compound called a flushing or finishing solution, in order to rid all excess nutrients and chemicals from the vegetation prior to harvest; *flushing* must be done a minimum of one week prior to harvest in order to ensure the healthiest and tastiest buds; well-grown cannabis is *flushed* for five to fourteen days with a carbohydrate and/or magnesium solution and then a final seven to ten days with pure water; unflushed cannabis tastes harsh and metallic, often sparking in the bowl after combustion, and leaves a deep black ash remaining; also, *flushing* is what you are doing with your money if you buy cheap, dirty, unchelated petroleum-based synthetic hydroponic nutrients for use in cannabis cultivation

flushing solution (finishing solution)- *n.* a specialized hydroponic nutrient solution designed to remove excess fertilizers and eliminate salt buildup; typically, a *flushing solution* is nothing more than a one to five percent magnesium sulfate (Epsom salt) solution occasionally mixed with a carbohydrate source like glucose syrup and a color tracer; at twenty to fifty dollars per liter, most *flushing solutions* are a waste of money considering the fact that a large container of OMRI Epsom salts retails for about fifteen dollars and distilled water is less than a dollar a gallon; believe it or not, some hydroponic growers actually use flavored or scented *finishing solutions*... the fact that people use these products (and that companies produce them) perfectly illustrates the ignorance and immorality of the typical cannabis clown: there are cannabis varieties that naturally taste like the flavors, and smell like the aromas, the finishers are supposed to imitate; if pineapple or grape is desired, find a strain having that terpene profile instead of turning the cannabis into fake plastic trees

flyin'- *adj. see high*

foliar- *adj.* of or relating to cannabis leaves; —*n. see foliar spray*

foliar feed- *v.* to spray a nutrient solution directly on cannabis leaves for immediate or near immediate absorption and availability to the plant; *foliar feeding* should only be done with safe, organic materials approved for foliar use on cannabis, and at early morning or right before horticultural lighting is illuminated, and should never be performed after the second or third week of flowering

foliar spray- *n.* the solution used in foliar feeding

Forçade, Tom- *n.* a cannabis legend and the illustrious creator of the preeminent cannabis magazine, *High Times*

force (force flowering)- *v.* to induce flowering of mature cannabis plants by reducing the available light to any photoperiod less than thirteen and a half hours for most strains; typically, *force flowering* refers to reducing the light cycle to twelve-twelve; —*n.* the act of or process of *force flowering;* this is not to be confused with the mythological power that infuses semi-intellectual, role-playing outcasts and allows them to perform their inexplicably intense superhero power of repelling members of the opposite sex

fork- *n.* a pronged dab tool used for stabbing shatter; also, the characteristic state of a reformer's tongue and his striking resemblance to a prohibitionist politician

forum cut- *n.* a cannabis cutting or clone procured specifically on the cannabis forums; most often, *forum cut* refers specifically to the cutting of *Girl Scout Cookies* that was being passed around on a popular forum; *i.e. Don't waste your time or money trying to get a forum cut when it's likely the same as the GSC clone at your local dispensary.*

forum handle- *n.* the equivalent to a breeder handle for forum members, but less important and more juvenile; *see breeder handle*

forums- *n.pl.* the collective group comprised of the multiple online cannabis cultivation, breeding, and genetics exchange *forums* that sprouted up during total prohibition as a way for cannabis-friendly people to connect, share wisdom and genetics, and talk mad fucking shit about each other and everyone else; to real cannabis cultivators and breeders who spend every waking moment of every day of the year working or planning their cannabis gardens, the *forums* are somewhat of a joke… especially considering how much misinformation spreads there like a venereal disease at a prostitute-sex-addict's conference

four-footer- *n.* a specific type of bong so named for the fact that it is four feet tall from base to orifice; *four-footer* is not to be confused with Chris Hemsworth's cock

fragrant cane- *n. see kaneh bosom*

Franco- *n.* one of the current head breeders for Green House Seed Co. and Strain Hunters

Frenchy (Frenchy Cannoli)- *n.* a French hashmaker and true extract artist now based out of Northern Cali who is famous for his cannoli; *see cannoli*

fresh air exchange- *n.* a system of ventilation and atmosphere supplementation in an indoor grow operation that utilizes fans and ducting to exchange the air in the room with outside air at set, periodic intervals; in places where temperatures are not regularly subfreezing, a *fresh air exchange* system is far superior to a closed system operating a CO_2 generator

frizzled (frizzazled)- *adj.* having the characteristic of being extremely high, especially while wearing bright bedazzled pasties and chaps and dancing to Gloria Gaynor songs with your beautiful buttery boys

fucked- *adj.* a fucking colloquial fucking term used to describe the fuck someone feels from fucking their fucking shit up with some motherfuckin' cannabis that's so *fucked* it's the fuckin' fuck no other fuckers have ever been fucked-up on… know what the fuck I'm fuckin' sayin'?

full extract cannabis oil (FECO)- *n.* a cannabis extract made by refluxing or washing high potency cannabis flowers in ethanol and reducing the resulting liquid into an essential oil of whole-plant cannabis; there are many recipes for *full extract cannabis oil* that use harmful and toxic chemicals like naphtha, toluene or benzene and are not considered by anyone with any fucking common sense to be safe for human consumption; *for differentiation, see Milagro oil, Obsidian Oil, Rick Simpson Oil, Phoenix Tears*

full-melt- *adj.* of or having the characteristic of a cannabis concentrate that completely melts or vaporizes upon the application of heat instead of combusting or charcoaling; —*full melt n.* a cannabis concentrate that exhibits the quality of fully melting; —*melt v.* what my mind did when I sold over a million copies of *The Doobieous Dictionary* in a week

fungicide- *n.* a pesticide specifically designed to combat issues with a variety of fungi that can infest or have infested a cannabis plant or its medium; *fungicide* is not to be confused with the homicide of your joy committed by parents or prohibitionists

fungus gnats- *n.pl.* small, dark flies of the Sciaridae family that feast on cannabis; the adults spread diseases like tobacco mosaic virus from plant to plant; the larvae ravenously eat cannabis roots; when I had a problem with *fungus gnats*, I was told by a botanist that the only way to truly eradicate them was "to move. Leave everything there to burn to the ground, including the clothes on your back," which I did

fyah- *n. see fire*

ganja (ganj)- *n.* cannabis flower as opposed to *bhang*; *ganja* is not a colloquial term for cannabis, but is actually the Sanskrit word for *hemp* that ultimately became Hindi for *the cut and dried flowering tops of the cannabis plant; ganja* is spelled with a *j*, not a *g*... *ganga* is a bastardization of *gang of* used as a collective term to signify a large quantity of something; *i.e. I gotta ganga ganja in my homie's garage.*

ganjapreneur- *n.* the somewhat derogatory contemporary coinage assigned to an entrepreneur in the cannabis industry or in the ancillary cannabis products market

gangsta lean- *v.* to inadvertently tilt one's body slightly to an angle after consuming large quantities of cannabis, especially while listening to beats; —*n.* the result of such action; *i.e. I got my gangsta lean on from some Cali shit while some valley chick put the sheen on my tip.*

Garlic Bud- *n.* a legendary *Afghani* strain from the 1990s that has an intense, sharp musky aroma reminiscent of garlic; some have speculated that the *Chemdog* line is a descendant of the *Garlic Bud*; a bred version of the strain is *Shiva Shanti* by Sensi Seeds

gas chromatography- *n.* an archaic method of testing the chemical composition of cannabis sample materials that is unfortunately still being employed by contemporary cannabis labs; in regards to cannabis, *gas chromatography* is the least accurate, and somewhat of a joke; anyone wanting to have their cannabis samples tested needs to ensure that the cannabis lab uses liquid chromatography or spectroscopy, not *gas chromatography*; *i.e. Due to the issue of heat induced decarboxylation, gas chromatography is worthless in virtually all cannabis testing applications. It's like burning down a house and analyzing the ash in order to determine what program was playing on the television that used to be inside.*

gas mask- *n.* a type of smoking apparatus that goes over the nose and mouth, or the entire head, and resembles the military gas masks of wars past, presumably as a sardonic social criticism of the poisoning of society and its defiant refusal of healing wind

gateway drug- *n.* in nearly one hundred percent of the cases, caffeine, alcohol, pharmaceutical medications (both OTC and prescription), sugar, chocolate, or tobacco; the term fallaciously given to cannabis because of the claim that it is supposed to lead to the use of harder drugs; if this is the case, please show me the person who never consumed any drug, including aspirin, caffeine, alcohol or tobacco, and just one day smoked cannabis which led to sucking dick in back alleys for crack... that person just doesn't exist; *i.e. I have never been hanging around after smokin' bowls and thought, hey, maybe I'll go do some heroin... it's so much fun and so safe! It's actually pretty safe to say that cannabis is not a gateway drug.*

gateway effect- *n.* the debatable concept that one thing begets another; in logical fallacies, the *gateway effect* is often called snowballing or false cause and effect; in terms of cannabis, it is the erroneous belief that consuming cannabis will beget the use of dangerous drugs; *see gateway drug*

GDP- *abbrv. see Granddaddy Purple*

gear- *n.* collectively, any cannabis and the tools required for its consumption

generalized fertilizers (all-purpose)- *n.pl.* the group of liquid or granular synthetic fertilizers or blends that are designed for broad applications as opposed to cannabis cultivation; *generalized fertilizers* are ubiquitously found under familiar brand names in the aisles of every single gardening super center monstrosity or other hardware store as they are often used for supposed miraculous growth of tomatoes and flowers; for many reasons, *generalized fertilizers* should never be used to feed cannabis

genetic hoarding- *n.* the act of depriving future generations of unique, special, or rare cannabis strains, and of stealing from current patients in need; *genetic hoarding* is being practiced by forum members, large CBD or other commercial producers, and dispensaries in order to protect their rights to a monopoly on a market for a specific trend or rarity; *i.e. Unfortunately, the world has lost some of its greatest strains. The capitalistic douche bags on the forums, who don't know the least bit about cultivating cannabis, are the most guilty of genetic hoarding and the most likely to lose the strain to some sort of plague, infestation, or raid.*

genetics- *n.pl.* cannabis seeds; also, *genetics* refers to the title and origins of a particular strain; when citing a strain's *genetics*, the following format is the industry standard in the US (the UK often lists the father first, but that's their misogynistic prerogative): *Strain Name (Mother Name x Father's Name); i.e. For the rest of our sakes, I wish the poser breeders and pollen slingers would actually cite their strains' genetics correctly.*

genotype- *n.* when it comes to cannabis, think about it like this: the *genotype* is the strain, variety or landrace itself, and the phenotype is a specific plant of that variety; true-breeding *genotypes* of cannabis will produce virtually no variation in offspring, regardless of filial generation or quantity sown; unstable *genotypes* will have a great deal of variety, and present with multiple different phenotypes beginning at filial generation one

get high- *v.* to consume cannabis for the ultimate effect of achieving euphoria, enlightenment or orgasm; to *get high* is not to be confused with to *get low*, which is practiced in the proverbial bedroom or on the dance floor and can also lead to orgasm

getting high on your own supply- *phr.* the description given to the practice of using one's own cultivated or procured cannabis to get high as opposed to purchasing cannabis from a dispensary, buying it from a dealer, or borrowing it from a friend; this phrase can have both positive and negative connotations, depending on usage: when a private citizen can achieve this state, she is afforded an increase of available income and the peace of mind and satisfaction of consuming self-grown cannabis… however, when *getting high on your own supply* is practiced by a dealer, he is afforded a loss of profit, customer base, and, depending on his justification in the local hierarchy, potentially his life

Ghost OG- *n.* an indica dominant hybrid (or phenotype) of *OG Kush* supposedly bred by OrgnKid and released to the world by a forum breeder with the handle, Ghost; *Ghost OG* is believed to be an offspring or cultivar of *Triangle Kush* out of Florida in the 1990s; some people believe the *Ghost* cut to be the mother cut of all OGs; *for disambiguation, see OG Kush*

gibberellins- *n.pl.* a group of plant hormones responsible for regulating growth and certain developmental processes, including gender expression; *gibberellins* are used on female cannabis plants by large commercial breeding companies to create reversed pollen to use for making feminized hybrids

ginger- *n.* the rhizomatous spice, Zingiber *officinale,* that supposedly enhances the effects of THC when consumed concurrently with cannabis use or consumption; according to lore, the terpenes and blood-thinning compounds in common foods like *ginger* add to the entourage effect induced by whole-plant cannabis consumption; in the case of *ginger*, its use is said to aid in the absorption of orally administered cannabis and increase or amplify its effects

ginger bud- *n.* a general colloquialism for cannabis flowers that are excessively coated in orange or red hairs; *i.e. Hey look! That redhead has a buncha ginger bud! Hahaha… what a funny coincidence!*

Girl Scout Cookies- *n.* an indica dominant cannabis strain supposedly created by a breeding collective out of Northern California and Florida called The Cookie Family that is *OG Kush x F1 x Durban Poison*; reportedly, knockoffs of the strain called by the same name are actually *OG Kush x Durban Poison x Cherry Pie* bred by The Hemp Center, or an *OG Kush x GDP x Cherry Pie* knockoff by somebody in Oakland, and are not in fact the real *Girl Scout Cookies*; *i.e. The real knockoffs of Girl Scout Cookies are fuckin' yummy... but knockoffs of the SF and Oakland knockoffs are not so funny, and posers should knock it the fuck off.*

glandular trichomes- *n.pl. see trichomes*

glass- *n.* a dangerous colloquial term for the solvent-extracted cannabis concentrate *shatter;* unfortunately, *glass* is yet another incident where weed wackos have adopted the name of a dangerous synthetic drug for something cannabis related; in this case, the name and coinciding danger may actually be clear; also, *glass* can refer to a glass smoking device like a pipe or bong; *i.e. Look at that guy... he's dabbin' some glass through his favorite glass.*

glass-on-glass- *adj.* having the characteristic of a junction or union, as on a bong or percolator, that uses a glass-to-glass connection to create an airtight seal; most often, top quality bongs or glass pieces are constructed with *glass-on-glass* connections so that there are no synthetic parts, like grommets, employed in the device

glassy eyes- *n.pl.* a stereotypical side effect of ingesting cannabis and the main reason certain eye drop brands remained in business throughout the last thirty years

glob- *n.* an extremely large dab

globe- *n. see dome*

glycerin- *n.* vegetable *glycerin*; a natural byproduct from the cultivation and processing of plant material that is extremely sweet and exceptionally viscous; *glycerin* is classified as a sugar alcohol that is used as an edible solvent and the base for non-alcoholic tinctures (solutions); it should be consumed with a large glass of water when taken internally and should be avoided in quantity due to the potential of dehydration, among other side effects

God's Gift- *n.* an indica dominant cannabis strain that is *Granddaddy Purple x OG Kush*; what cannabis is to humanity

going bowling- *phr.* a common euphemism for smoking bowls of cannabis; *i.e. Be careful if you decide to ask your colleagues to go bowling with you in Colorado… they may just bring an unexpected sunshine surprise to the party.*

Golden Goat- *n.* a sativa dominant cannabis strain bred in Topeka, Kansas, that is a cross of *Island Sweet Skunk x Hawaiian Romulan* and gets her name from the local recycling center; *Golden Goat* is one of those strains that is truly unique on the scene, not just another me, too, and is deserving of all the accolades endlessly lauded upon lesser, tired strains like those from the GSC family; *i.e. Anyone want to share a cutting of Golden Goat with me? I would be very grateful!*

gone- *adj. see faded*

goo- *n.* any sticky concentrate like budder or taffy; what's left on your face after a night partying with your boys

good ol' buds club- *phr.* the name assigned to the current cannabis community and market due to the inordinate number of men over women participating in the cultivation and fair showing of cut flowers; slowly, the *good ol' buds club* is being infiltrated with the effects of affirmative action, and we are seeing numerous ambitious feminists leaving the board room or kitchen to enter the industry; rock on, ladies… you're raisin' the bar (unlike the bud bimbos who are dancin' on it)

goods- *n.pl.* colloquial for cannabis or illegal drugs

good stuff- *n.* great quality cannabis; *i.e. Hey man, y'all got the goods? 'Fuck yeah, I always got the good stuff, yo.'*

goo goo doll- *n.* an endearing and sexist euphemism for a female dabber, especially one who trolls after a Dhead with a big tackle box full of extracts and is willing to go head over heels for a D

Gorilla Glue #4- n. an extremely potent sativa dominant cannabis strain bred by Joesy Whales (Josey Wales) that is *Sour Dubb x Chem Sis x Chocolate Diesel;* the only glue that's safe to huff

GPM- *abbrv.* gallons per minute

gram- *n.* one twenty-eighth of an ounce; cannabis is sold by the gram, by increments of eighths of an ounce, or by the pound (leave it to dumbshit stoners to mix metric and imperial systems of measures); a *gram* of medical cannabis retails for between five and thirty dollars, though it costs fractions of a cent to produce

Granddaddy Purple- n. an indica dominant cannabis strain from California that was popularized by Ken Estes; supposedly, *Granddaddy Purple* is the hybrid or phenotype of *Mendo Purps* from which such famous strains as *Grape Ape and Purple Erkle* were developed; *see Mendo Purps*

Grandma's Boy- n. a pro-cannabis film released in 2006 that actually presents a fairly realistic, albeit hyperbolic and satirical, portrayal of cannabis and the illicit industry

Grannies for Grass- *n.* a grassroots organization based out of Illinois, Ohio and Missouri comprised of pro-cannabis grandparents and sympathetic citizens; *i.e. Get on with your badass selves, Grannies for Grass! Respect.*

Grape Ape- n. see Granddaddy Purple

grass- *n.* an old school term for cannabis

gravity bong- *n.* a specific type of bong that actually uses capillarity and water pressure, not gravity, to function; a *gravity bong* consists of a bottomless chamber that has been submerged in a basin or pail of water and has a bowl attached to the top filled with cannabis; smoke fills the chamber of the *gravity bong* as it is lifted out of the water in conjunction with combustion of the buds in the bowl; then, one removes the bowl and inhales the entire volume of cannabis smoke often by forcing the chamber back in the water to cause the smoke to rush in the lungs

Great White- *n.* a specific brand of microbiological soil or nutrient additive from Plant Success that is considered by many to be the industry standard for microbiological applications

green- *n.* a color; the emotion other people feel when they see my flowers; *the green* is the first hit of a bowl; when smoking in a group and you are given *the green* hit, it is considered polite to only spark part of the bowl; if there are four or less people smoking, etiquette dictates that you divide *the green* equally; — *adj.* in reference to bud, *green* bud is the best; in this day and age, anyone selling you brown weed that isn't chocolate covered is as dirty as their buds look

Green Belt- *n.* the prospector and journalists' coinage for the region spanning from Washington through Oregon and California over to Colorado; occasionally, some will refer to the *Green Belt* as the area spanning from Alaska through Canada all the way to Colorado, or the entirety of the United Kingdom and their slowly softening stance on cannabis; *Green Belt* is not to be confused with the hued strap used to identify the advancement or graduation of one's fear or sadism in the arts of violence

green bud (greenbud)- *n.* see green; —*California Greenbud n.* the best cannabis in the entire world; *i.e. California Greenbud has been diluted by the influx of out-of-state ganjapreneurs who mistakenly think they can grow well simply because they crossed the border.*

green goddess- *n.* deferential colloquialism for cannabis, especially high-potency cannabis flowers… because everyone knows a goddess has a sweet and intoxicating flower

green gold- *n.* a colloquial term for cannabis based on its market value; also, *green gold* can refer to cover crops; *i.e. I plant a bunch of different types of green gold to till in to feed my green gold in the spring and summer.*

greenhouse (green house)- *adj.* of or relating to outdoor cannabis that was cultivated in an agricultural *greenhouse* instead of completely outside; according to common perception, the breakdown in cannabis flower quality is as follows: 1. indoor, 2. outdoor, 3. *greenhouse*, OR 1. indoor, 2. *greenhouse*, 3. outdoor; however, *greenhouse* cannabis can be the best quality due to having the environmental benefits of both indoor and outdoor cultivation; —*n.* the place in which *greenhouse* cannabis is grown

Green House Seed Co.- *n.* one of the oldest and most commercial cannabis breeding companies in the Netherlands; *see Arjan, Franco*

Green Rush- *n.* the clever, journalistic buzz phrase used to describe the explosion of businesses and financial opportunities, like a new cannabis publishing market, that are cropping up all across areas sympathetic to cannabis in legal states; *i.e. My buddy got in on the Green Rush by inventing a rosin extracting device, and now he is a multimillionaire.*

grind- *v.* to break apart cannabis flowers into smaller pieces using a small canister in which set tines are housed and designed to slice through the vegetative cannabis material as the top and bottom lids are rotated in opposite directions; *grinding* is only recommended when the cannabis flowers are going to be rolled in a joint or packed into an oven, and is usually unnecessary when smoking from a bong or pipe (depending on bud density)

grinder- *n.* the device used to grind cannabis flowers prior to smoking or vaping

Grinspoon, Lester- *n.* an Associate Professor Emeritus at Harvard University, and former senior psychiatrist at the

Massachusetts Mental Health Center in Boston, who is famous for being a cannabis prohibitionist until he did scientific studies to determine that he had been entirely wrong, that cannabis is in fact a healthy, beneficial plant; due to his conversion and pro-cannabis work, Barney's Farm bred and named a sativa strain after *Dr. Grinspoon*, dubbing it "the thinking man's sativa"

grizz- *n.* colloquial for a gram; *i.e. Real cannabis smokers don't buy the shit by the grizz, they buy their shit by the ozzy or grow it themselves.*

grommet- *n.* the rubber ring that holds the seal between the body and the slide of a bong, or between the slide and the stem

grow- *v.* to cultivate cannabis; when *grow* is added to the word *up*, it is what the author of this book needs to do; —*n.* the formula of hydroponic nutrient designed specifically for the vegetative cycle, or that contains the macronutrients typically necessary for growing cannabis that is used in conjunction with another formula or formulas in multi-part nutrient formulations

grow bags- *n.pl.* the containers designed for cannabis cultivation that are soft sided and more baglike than the traditional hard plastic containers; *grow bags* are often constructed of recycled fibers and fabrics

grow op (grow operation)- *n.* any cannabis cultivation done for more than personal use; often, *grow op* refers to a large (illegal) commercial cannabis cultivation operation; usually, one would not refer to her own personal garden as a *grow op* unless she was personally growing for the entire neighborhood

grow stones- *n.pl. see recycled glass stones;* also, the term *grow stones* refers to a group of silica-rich volcanic glass rocks that are used in hydroponic cultivation and as a soil amendment

grow tent (grow hut)- *n. see indoor greenhouse*

Grow the Cure, Sow the Love- *phr.* a succinct mantra developed by Love Genetics that is used to remind oneself that the cure to all illness yet remains in *love*, and the more we sow it, the more we all heal

GSC- *abbrv. see Girl Scout Cookies*

guano- *n.* politically correct shit specifically designed to be disseminated in the garden uprising

guerilla grow- *v.* to cultivate cannabis illegally, especially on public property or someone else's land; —*n.* an illegal outdoor cannabis farm on public or forest service land; *i.e. Anyone who decides to guerilla grow remember this: three people were just shot to death, because they were caught doing this on a rancher's land.*

Gupta, Sanjay- *n.* the lead medical correspondent for CNN and noted former radical prohibitionist turned cannabis reformer; *Dr. Gupta's* media exposés on the benefits of cannabis, especially medical cannabis, have helped bring a positive perspective to mainstream US citizens

hack- *v.* to cough violently and ferociously after taking an inhalation of cannabis smoke or vapor

hack up a lung- *phr.* the metaphorical outcome of consuming poorly grown, harsh cannabis or smoking through dirty bong water or an unclean implement; the painful, hypothetical eventuality of hacking; *see hack*

Haight-Ashbury- *n.* an infamous borough or district of San Francisco located at the intersection of Haight and Ashbury streets that was one of the many birthplaces of the hippie culture, and was highly congregated during The Summer of Love

hair straightener- *n.* the beautician's device often used by stylish cannabis dabbers who want to participate in the latest trendy fad of making and consuming rosin; *see rosin*

hairs- *n.pl. see pistils*

hairy- *adj.* having the quality of cannabis flowers that have an excessive amount of hairs; *i.e. The hairy lady always has hairy buds for sale out of an ice chest at the local farmers market.*

half- *n.* an amount of cannabis equivalent to one half of an ounce

half-baked- *adj.* having the quality of nearly high or stoned, but not quite all the way there; *half-baked* is also the perfect description of cannabis laws and legislation, like CCHI, MCLR and the Adult Use of Marijuana Act

Half-Baked- *n.* a ridiculous and derogatory cannabis movie that is equivalent to the racist films of the past that had bigots...er...actors dressed in blackface guffawing around as hyperbolic and stereotypical caricatures of "negroes"; *Half-Baked* is one long commercial for prohibition and is astonishingly offensive to any cannabis person with class; to the film and the filmmakers, I say this: pussy is great... pot is great... but the two are way better together... if the bitch truly loved Thurgood, she would have been down with smokin' the sacred cannabis and then fuckin' his brains out

hammer- *n.* a specific type of cannabis pipe or bubbler that gets its name from the fact that its shape bears resemblance to a *hammer* (though, now that I provide this definition, I must pause to ponder whether or not most cannabis clowns have ever used a real hammer or even know what the fuck one is)

handle- *n. see breeder handle, forum handle*

happy cake- *n. see space cake*

Harborside Health Center- *n.* one of the largest, and possibly the most notorious and infamous, medical cannabis dispensaries in the nation that is co-owned by Steve DeAngelo; with two California Bay Area locations, they are also likely one of the wealthiest dispensaries

hardener- *n.* a flower *hardener* is nothing more than a synthetic nutrient solution designed for cannabis cultivation that has extremely elevated levels of phosphorus and potassium and a complete absence of nitrogen

hardening- *v. see harden off;* also, the arterial condition easily reversed by a simple wife-swap between alcohol and cannabis in one's life-movie

harden off- *v.* to slowly transition and strengthen a cannabis cutting or seedling in preparation for placing it under direct sunlight or under intense horticultural lighting

Harlequin- *n.* a clone-only cannabis strain bred by Wade Laughter that is a hybrid of *Columbian Gold*, a *Laos Thai*, a Swiss sativa, and a *Nepali*; *Harlequin* is known for her proportionally high level of CBD to THC, but often has a low total cannabinoid profile of 13-15%

Harold and Kumar- *n.* the authentic, though often grievously hyperbolic, stoner characters of the eponymous movie trilogy who celebrate cannabis and its recreational use

Harrelson, Woody- *n.* an actor known for his role in the celebrated sitcom, *Cheers,* his quirky parts in movies, and his open, public advocacy for cannabis

harsh- *adj.* the term used to describe cannabis that causes fits of coughing, burning lungs, or has a caustic smoke and flavor; *harsh* cannabis is typically caused by an excess or buildup of hydroponic nutrients, or by being cured or stored improperly; *i.e. Much of the cannabis available commercially is rather harsh. The growers purposefully don't flush out the hydroponic nutrients so that the heavy metals help make the flowers weigh as much as possible.*

hash- *abbrv. see hashish*

hash bar- *n.* supposedly, a bar on the beach specifically designed for people to buy and consume hash or cannabis; also, a bar of soap with hash or kief added prior to saponification

hash brownie- *n. see magic brownie*

hash caps- *n.pl.* cannabis caps made specifically with hashish; *see caps*

hashish- *n.* a specific type of cannabis extract where the sticky resins and glandular trichome heads are forcibly removed from the cannabis plant material; *hashish* is also the origin of the word *assassin* due to the fact that, during the time of the Crusades, a *hashishiyyin* ("hash-eater") named Hassan-i Sabbah would murder his enemies after intoxicating them with edible hash; common types of *hashish* are *finger hash*, where the hash is rubbed from the flowers by hand; *bubble hash*, where the hash is extracted in ice water; and *stripper hash*, where people run through the fields nude in order to strip off the trichomes from the still-producing plants

hashmaker (hash maker)- *n.* one who makes hashish; a less respected term for one who makes concentrates; *for differentiation, see extract artist*

hash pipe- *n.* a pipe with a special bowl and elongated shaft designed specifically for smoking or vaping hashish

hash press- *n.* a specific type of table-top press, usually hydraulic, that is used to form medallions, bricks or pucks of hash

hash puck- *n.* a medallion or cube of hash that has been pressed or formed together; typically, a *hash puck* weighs one eighth to one ounce and often bears the seal or emblem of the hashmaker

hashtag (hash tag)- *n.* the moronic contemporary term for a pound sign that social media dimwits invented because they had no idea the character already had a designation; *i.e. The only hashtag I'm interested in is a pound of bubble!;* hashtag is not to be confused with the exorbitant price charged for the resinous secretions of a weed

Hawaiian- *n.* a hybrid cannabis landrace from Hawaii

Hawaiian Snow- *n.* a sativa dominant cannabis strain bred by Green House Seed Co. that is a cross of a *Hawaiian* sativa and a *Laos; Hawaiian Snow's* claim to fame is that she truly smells and tastes of sweet and sour chives, and is excellent in savory culinary applications

hay- *n.* colloquial for cannabis, especially flowers that are leafy or immature

Haze (Original Haze)- *n.* a sativa dominant cannabis strain bred by the Haze Brothers in Santa Cruz, California, that is a polyhybrid cross of *Mexican, Columbian, Thai,* and *Indian* cannabis landraces; also, the main character of one of the greatest cannabis series of all time, *The Unrevealed*

Headband- n. an indica dominant cannabis hybrid bred by…
uh… this is yet another one of those strains claimed by everyone,
so let's just say bred by the universe that is purported to be *Sour
Diesel x OG Kush* or *NYC Diesel x OG Kush x Master Kush*; the
strain also goes by the names *Sour Kush, 707 Headband and 818
Headband* depending on who *bred* it; supposedly, the original
Headband is from the 707 area code in San Francisco and is so
named after a headband due to the effect smoking *Headband* the
strain produces on the brain

head change- *n.* the transitory and vaguely quantifiable state of
being during the brief instant that one goes from being sober to
feeling the effects of cannabis consumption

head shop- *n.* an establishment that legally distributes cannabis
paraphernalia and ancillary goods specific to smoking, dabbing,
or vaping; a *head shop* carries rigs, pipes, bongs, hookahs,
papers, blunt wraps and replacement parts for all sorts of
implements; a cannabis *head shop* is not to be confused with an
establishment that sells blow jobs, for those are only legal in the
pious and conservative Nevada (a mostly deserted suburb of Los
Angeles)

heady- *adj.* having the quality or producing the sensation of
cannabis-induced euphoria as opposed to sedation

heat- *n.* colloquial for fucking hot cannabis flowers

heavy metal toxicity- *n.* the condition of being poisoned through
ingestion of leafy green plants and vegetables, like tea, spinach,
cannabis and kale, that have been cultivated in soil with excess
levels of certain poisonous trace metals; *heavy metal toxicity* is
the primary reason to never fertilize or feed cannabis plants trace
minerals unless there is a documented nutrient deficiency, and a
great excuse to never have to eat kale

heirloom cannabis- *n.* any cannabis cultivar or variety that has
been passed down for generations, either by asexual propagation

or stabilized hybrid seed; *heirloom cannabis* is often regional or location specific with greater expansion and availability only now beginning due to legalization efforts; examples of *heirloom cannabis* are *Maui Wowie, Northern Lights, Silver Pearl; for differentiation, see landrace cannabis*

hemp- *n.* the common name given to the variety of sativa cannabis plants that are low in cannabinoids, high in fiber for textiles; *hemp* is classified as Cannabis *sativa Linnaeus* (Cannabis *sativa l.)* due to the fact that taxonomist Carl Linnaeus believed all cannabis to be hemp; Linnaeus was unaware of the differences in landraces and drug strains versus European hemp or textile strains; since Linnaeus' error, the taxonomic nomenclature of the Cannabis genus has been adjusted to include drug varietals and landrace species (*indica, ruderalis, sativa*), and now common usage employs the classification Cannabis *sativa l.* to only designate hemp or textile strains; this makes the wording of the Adult Use of Marijuana Act highly confusing… are they really trying to legalize recreational hemp?; *for differentiation, see cannabis, indica, sativa, ruderalis*

hemp oil- *n.* a byproduct of cannabis textile production that is often heavily contaminated with industrial lubricants and toxic solvents, and is pawned off on unsuspecting and desperate parents as a source of CBD that is *legal* in all fifty states; certain villainous companies have tried to capitalize on the suffering and ignorance of the parents of terminally ill or epileptic children by conning them into believing that ineffective *hemp oil* is the same as high CBD full extract cannabis oil; for the record, industrial *hemp oil* or paste is not high in cannabinoids, as the federal government has established extremely low legal guidelines for total cannabinoid content in hemp products like hempseed oil and hulled hempseed; that means, the companies are telling you a half truth: yes, their oil is legal in the US, but no it is not high in CBD or THC, or vice versa; *i.e. To any parent in need of true full extract cannabis oil, avoid hemp oil and the horrible hustlers slangin' that shit, move to Colorado, Oregon, or California, and save your baby with real full extract medical cannabis oil.*

hempseed- *n.* the seed from the Cannabis *sativa Linnaeus* plant that is consumed as one of the world's most nutritious and healthy food and food oil sources; *hempseed* is high in Omega-6, Omega-3, Omega-9, potassium, protein, iron, thiamine, niacin, B6, folate, phosphorous, magnesium, copper and manganese; not only is *hempseed* invaluable as a world food source, it also is a great organic amendment or fertilizer for growing drug strains of cannabis

hempseed oil (hemp seed oil)- *n.* culinary cannabis oil made from cold-pressed cannabis seeds that is nonpsychoactive and extremely nutritious; *hempseed oil* is high in beneficial fatty acids, with the ideal three to one ratio of Omega-6 to Omega-3; it contains Super Omega-3 (SDA) and Super Omega-6 (GLA), both of which assist or aid the body in metabolizing fat… imagine that, cannabis seeds produce a fat that is so healthy it helps reduce unhealthy fats in the human body

hempwick (hemp wick)- *n.* a cord of hemp often coated in beeswax that is ignited in order to be used to combust cannabis flowers or concentrates; a supposedly safer and healthier alternative to a lighter; *i.e. Our culture would be extremely different had there been such classics as the Witches of Hempwick or The Hempwick Chronicles.*

herb (herbal)- *n.* old school for cannabis; hey, isn't that your dealer's name, too?

herbalista- *n.* a female who consumes cannabis; also, *herbalista* is a casual name for a female budtender; —*herbalist n.* a male *herbalista*

Herbies Seeds- *n.* a UK-based cannabis seed bank that is known for shipping to countries worldwide; *Herbies* is The Attitude's main competition

Herer, Jack- *n.* the author of *The Emperor Wears No Clothes: Hemp and the Marijuana Conspiracy,* and celebrated cannabis legend; singularly one of the most mispronounced names in the history of cannabis, and it seems to be incorrectly spoken by very specific groups of people: weed snobs, New York pretentious elitists, and Cali poser dispensary punks (how old are you, like 18 going on 12?); for the record, it is pronounced like *hair er*, not *her AIR;* her air is your greezy girlfriend's flatulence

herm- *abbrv. see hermaphrodite*

hermaphrodite- *n.* a cannabis plant that expresses the gender traits of both male and female flowers; cannabis is naturally always striving to be a perfect plant in order to ultimately perpetuate the species, and there will be the occasional *hermaphrodite* in the offspring of most parents

hermaphroditic- *adj.* having the characteristics of a hermaphrodite

hermie- *n. see hermaphrodite*

heroin quotient- *n.* the hypothetical statistical result of the potential reduction in the number of hospitalizations and deaths of people who used heroin or other opiates based on substituting cannabis as a replacement; a high *heroin quotient* in an area means a large number of heroin, opiate, or prescription pain medication related deaths that could have been avoided with cannabis use; a low *heroin quotient* in an area suggests a greater tolerance or acceptance of cannabis, especially medical cannabis, as evidenced by fewer of these deaths; *i.e. Studies have repeatedly shown that the heroin quotient and prescription medication abuse significantly drop in areas with legal recreational and medical cannabis.*

HID (HID lighting)- *abbrv. see high intensity discharge lighting*

high- *adj.* the most common colloquial term for being affected by cannabis; *high* originates in the fact that cannabis can get one closer to God; —*n. the high* is the euphoria experienced from cannabis consumption

high as a kite- *phr.* well, if this shit isn't as self-explanatory as a name tag, then I don't know a damn thing

high intensity discharge lighting (HID)- *n.* a specific type of horticultural lighting used in cannabis cultivation that refers to high pressure sodium and metal halide lamps; *see high pressure sodium, metal halide*

High Times Magazine- *n.* the preeminent, longest-running, cannabis-centered magazine available to the public; since its inception in 1974, *High Times Magazine* has been considered the authority on cannabis in the journalistic medium; cannabis pornography

high performance liquid chromatography (HPLC)- *n. see liquid chromatography*

Hindu- *n. see Hindu Kush*

Hindu Kush- *n.* a mountain range spanning Afghanistan and northern Pakistan from which *Kush* cannabis originates; the mountains also go by the names Caucasus Indicus (Ancient Greek), and Hindu Kash; this just goes to show you that indica and cash have been going hand in hand for thousands of years; —*n. Hindu Kush (Kush)* the indica dominant cannabis landrace from this region, or containing genetics from the strains in the area

hippie- *n.* the term given to members of the peace-loving, cannabis-friendly counterculture of the 1960s that is derived from the word *hipster* (ugh… it makes me cringe to be associated with a hipster-scene douche); *hippie* was popularized by journalist Herb Caen of *The San Francisco Chronicle*; the word is often offensively preceded by the word *dirty* to suggest that the lifestyle choice to celebrate peace, healthy living, happy homesteading, and love is somehow shameful or unclean; though I find far more filth in the lies hiding behind the eyes of the polished plastic kings and queens squeaking through the conservative scene; *hippie* is not to be confused with *hippy*, which is what your mom is

hippie hill- *n.* the place in nearly every major town or region where people can score some weed from a drug dealer

hit- *v.* to inhale a breath of cannabis smoke or vapor from a pipe, joint, bong, or other smoking or vaping device; often, *hit* is combined with a form of *to take* to make the verb, but not always; —*hit n.* an inhalation of cannabis smoke or vapor; *i.e. Hit this shit, muthafucka! I already done took a hit o' it, yo.; also, see hold it in*

hit the hay- *phr.* to smoke cannabis; *i.e. Be careful if your teen says she's going up to her room to hit the hay... she may just have gotten into your stash! You can't be havin' that... shiiit, bud's fuckin' expensive.*

HO- *abbrv.* the titular perception of your wife's sister; *also, see honey oil*

hoarder- *n.* one who practices genetic hoarding; *see genetic hoarding*

holding- *v.* illegally possessing cannabis, often for the purpose of sale

hold it in- *phr.* the phrase given to the common misconception that cannabis smoke needs to be held in the lungs for a long period of time in order to receive the benefits of the medicine or to get high; *hold it in* is a fallacy and is actually bad advice; the sensation of head rush and loss of consciousness are not from the cannabis, but rather a lack of oxygen to the brain; recent studies have shown that the optimal amount of time to *hold it in* is three seconds; *i.e. They say that I should only hold it in for three seconds? That's gonna be tough considering I'm still inhaling from the chamber after five!*

hollow stems- *n.pl.* a trait of certain cannabis plants in which the inside of the cylindrical stem where the pith would be is entirely hollow; urban legend has it that cannabis with *hollow stems* is somehow greater in cannabinoid or drug content, but experiential evidence suggests that stem density bears little or no correlation to the ultimate total cannabinoid profile of an individual plant (unless the strain itself has a low drug content like that of hemp)

honey- *n. see honey oil*

Honey Bee- *n. see Queen Bee Extractor*

honey bud- *n.* a cannabis flower that has been covered or dipped in honey oil; also, a *honey bud* is a luscious, scrumptious, beautiful and tasty pussy

honeycomb (honey comb)- *n.* a specific type of solvent-extracted concentrate that gets its name from the unique appearance in the final product after purging; the bubbles of off-gassing solvent leave dimples in the wax to make it *honeycomb*

honey oil (HO)- *n.* the name given to cannabis oil that has been extracted with a solvent like isopropyl alcohol or butane due to the fact that the resulting concentrate appears similar to honey in color, opacity, and consistency

hookah- *n.* a traditional oriental water pipe where smoke from coal-lit or coaled cannabis is drawn through the water using a tube or multiple tubes; although the *hookah* has been world renowned since before the days of the opium den, its contemporary, pop culture popularity was solidified by Lewis Carroll's character the *hookah* smoking caterpillar in *Alice's Adventures in Wonderland*

hookah bar (hookah-bar)- *n.* an establishment where users congregate to smoke *shisha*, a flavored tobacco blend; *hookah bars* will soon be converted to establishments for smoking cannabis through a hookah

hook up- *v.* to procure or to provide cannabis; when a pronoun is added, it means to direct cannabis towards someone specific; *i.e. Hook me up, wigga!;* —*n.* the person or place one can acquire cannabis; *i.e. I got the hook up, yo, and I can hook you up fat!*

hooter- *n.* a joint, pipe or other smoking device; the term *hooter* most likely comes from the correlation between taking in a drag of cannabis smoke and sucking on some shorty's nipples

horticultural lighting- *n.* the high output lighting used to cultivate cannabis plants indoors or in greenhouses; there are many quality types of horticultural lighting available to cannabis cultivators, including LED, HPS, plasma, MH, and (barely) fluorescent; *see LED, high pressure sodium, metal halide, fluorescent lighting, light emitting plasma*

hotbox (hot box)- *v.* to fill up a room or other small area with cannabis smoke such that the cloud is visible and remains without dissipating; —*hotboxed adj.* having the characteristic of a place that has been *hotboxed; i.e. That guy is so fuckin' legit he could hotbox the forest. 'Oh, you must be talkin' 'bout Jason Porter Collinsworth.'*

hot knife (hotknife)- *v.* to dab using a heated knife or blade as opposed to a nail; —*n.* the *hot knife* used to stab oneself with glass; *see stab*

house blend- *n.* the name applied by most dispensaries to the worst and least expensive cannabis flowers that they sell; *house blend* is synonymous with compassion shelf, but lacks the pretense; *for differentiation, see bottom shelf, compassion shelf, top shelf*

HPLC- *abbrv. see liquid chromatography*

HPS- *abbrv. see high pressure sodium*

Human Solution International, The- *n.* an organization that attempts to free nonviolent cannabis offenders from imprisonment, and helps prevent arrested citizens from ending up in jail for cannabis infractions

Humboldt County- *n.* the storied location of the world's greatest outdoor cannabis cultivation, or so they keep repeatedly reminding us; regardless, *Humboldt County* is partially responsible for supplying the entire US with the majority of its cannabis; *for differentiation, see Emerald Triangle, Mendocino County, Trinity County*

humic acid- *n.* the main component of the biodegraded organic constituents in fertile soil; *humic acid* is used as a soil conditioner, soil acidifier, microbiological activator, and nutrient transporter in soilless mixtures and mediums designed for cannabis cultivation

humidipack (humidipak)- *n.* a humidity packet designed to keep the relative humidity of a jar or canister at a set level, usually around sixty-two percent for cannabis

humulene- *n.* a common terpene found in cannabis that has a floral aroma; as it is one of the primary medical constituents of hops, *humulene* has undergone numerous scientific studies that have determined its efficacy as an anti-inflammatory; *humulene* is further proof that cannabis is indeed an invaluable medicine

humus- *n.* the raw, dark organic matter made from the decomposition of plant and animal materials that enriches a soil and provides nourishment and a healthy ecosystem for microbiologicals

hybrid (cross)- *n.* you; me; duh; the offspring of breeding two unique or different strains of cannabis

hydro- *abbrv. see hydroponic*

hydro store- *n.* a hydroponics retailer; a modern *barber shop* where (occasionally) gangsters and drug dealers (sometimes) hang out with il(legal) cannabis farmers; I quite literally overheard a conversation in a *hydro store* in Modesto where the clerk asked the guy how much money his dispensary made last year, and the motherfucker said, "Six million dollars tax-free"; I'm not joking and neither was he; and those evil greedy fuckers roll large while sick babies die because the medicine is too damn expensive... help me do something about this shit, please...

hydroponic- *adj.* grown unnaturally; —*n.* type of gardening where a neutral medium or substrate is used instead of soil, and nutrient solutions are added for nourishment; many *hydroponic* growers do not know how to grow and make two fatal mistakes: they overwater and overfeed; *hydroponics* can be done organically and all OMRI if the proper investment in time and money is taken; *hydroponic* and *indoor* are not synonymous; also, *hydroponic* is used as a colloquial term for any indoor or top-quality cannabis

IBL- *abbrv.* inbred backcross line; *see backcross*

ice- *n. see glass*

ice-water hash (ice hash)- *n. see bubble hash*

I'm cool- *phr.* a statement of satisfaction with one's current complete state of cannabis consumption, usually expressed to me at the end of the night when I'm still smoking and try to pass more of my buds to people who can barely remain awake

implement- *n.* any device that is used for the ingestion of cannabis smoke or vapor; *see bong, joint, piece, pipe, rig, etc.*

in a movie- *phr.* the description of the effect that many first time or novice cannabis users feel, especially in a social setting; often, a cannanewbie will be sitting in the corner at a party, *in a movie,* staring at everyone; *i.e. The first time I smoked Blueberry bud I was at a party and ended up in a movie, just sitting there crackin' the fuck up at all the fuckers fuckin' around.*

Indian- *n.* an indica cannabis landrace from India; can I just take a moment to say that there are some sincere *duh* entries in this dictionary... but, to my credit, I wanted to be sure that I was as inclusive as possible in all relative regards

indica- *n.* the species (or subspecies) of cannabis that originates from colder or higher elevation areas; *indicas* grow fat and full, tending more toward a bushlike plant structure; a common misconception is that *indicas* put a person down, while *sativas* pick a person up; rather, due to the common terpenes and the absence of THCv, *indicas* tend to be more relaxing and sedative than sativas; this leads to many of the more stereotypical stoner traits like couchlock, the munchies, and drowsiness; *for differentiation, see Cannabis*

indoor- *n.* any cannabis cultivated inside as opposed to outdoors or in a greenhouse; often fallaciously considered the best quality cannabis; due to this ignorant misconception, *indoor* cannabis is almost always more expensive than outdoor; if the outdoor is grown by an exceptional cannabis cultivator, it can be set side-by-side on the same shelf with *indoor* and fool almost all weed people; *hydroponic* and *indoor* are not synonymous, as soil-grown organic cannabis can be produced *indoors* with unbeatable results; no *indoor* hydro plant can top a comparable outdoor soil-grown plant in terms of flavor, aroma, nutrient and cannabinoid content, potency, and overall health and wellbeing of the plant, planet, patient and provider; —*adj.* having the quality of *indoor* cannabis

indoor greenhouse- *n.* a type of light-proof tent or hut that is designed to be used to cultivate cannabis in a small area inside a home or apartment

industrial cannabis- *n.* any cannabis or cannabis product intended for industrial or cosmetic use that is not intended for human consumption including but not limited to clothing, building materials, paper, fuels, fiber, plastics, lubricants, paints, animal feed, cosmetics, or lotions

inert- *adj. see neutral*

Initiative 502- *n.* the legislation in Washington state that legalized cannabis for adult recreational use, but criminalized personal medical use by forcing patients to enroll in a voluntary patient registry program and wear a green cross sewn onto their clothing if they want full access to their medicine; supposedly, at 81%, *Initiative 502* drew the largest voter turn out in history; *see voluntary patient registry*

inline fan- *n.* a type of fan that resides in the duct or duct path to boost flow or propel air through a carbon filter in the HVAC system of an indoor or greenhouse cannabis garden

insecticidal soap- *n.* a type of *natural* pest control measure that is basically lice shampoo for cannabis plants

intake filter- *n.* a specific type of duct filter that is employed in fresh air exchange systems as a means to prevent pests and problems from entering the indoor cannabis garden

internode (internode spacing, internode length)- *n.* the space between nodes on a cannabis plant; *internode spacing* is important to cannabis cultivation in regards to flower structure and overall yields

irie- *adj.* a Rastafarian Jamaican term that means high, pleasing, good, or nice; *i.e. Le's bi gettin' di bomb di make me irie.*

iron- *n. see dab tool*

ISO hash (ISO, ISO oil, QWISO)- *n.* a specific type of cannabis concentrate made by using ninety-one or ninety-nine percent isopropyl alcohol as the solvent; —*archaic* hash made using the method, and the Isomerizer machine, popularized by D. Gold in his informative cannabis chemistry manual, *Cannabis Alchemy*

ital- *n.* a specific type of food or culinary preparation practiced in Rastafarianism that often includes the use of cannabis flowers and parts as ingredients

J- *abbrv. see jay*

jacked- *adj. see fucked*

Jack Herer- *n.* a sativa dominant cannabis strain bred by Sensi Seeds that is a hybrid of *Skunk #1, Northern Lights #5* and *Haze;* the strain is named after "The Emperor", a cannabis and cultural hero; *see Herer, Jack*

Jamaican bake- *v.* to smoke or vape cannabis in a steamy shower or a sauna; *i.e. No shit, absolutely one of my favorite ways of smoking is to Jamaican bake a joint.*

jar- *n.* a glass container used to store cannabis flowers; possibly the most versatile, readily available and effective method of cannabis storage; cannabis stored in a *jar* should still be kept out of direct light and free from high temperatures or extreme temperature swings; possibly the best *jar* for storing cannabis is a UV (ultraviolet) protected, dark glass, like violetglass, with an airtight seal that has a humidipack added at the time the cured flowers are sealed

jay- *n.* colloquial for a joint; *i.e. Let's be like Matthew Arnold and smoke a jay of The White on the cliffs of Dover.*

Jay and Silent Bob- *n.* the fictional characters from the genius mind of Kevin Smith who were the inspiration for the fictional comic book characters, Bluntman and Chronic, in the Smithian film universe; *Jay and Silent Bob* were played by actor Jason Mewes and writer, director, actor Kevin Smith, respectively

jelly hash- *n.* a smokable cannabis concentrate comprised of hashish and cannabis oil

Jew Gold- *n.* an unknown cannabis indica hybrid of *OG Kush* and yet another example of the ignorant racism rampant among members of the cannabis community; this anti-Semitism should not be supported, and breeding companies and dispensaries selling *Jew Gold*, even if by the only-slightly-less-offensive pseudonym, *Kosher Kush,* should be avoided; this name is even more repulsive given the fact that Israel is the primary and preeminent country on the cutting edge of cannabis research and medical cannabis implementation; *i.e. Rumor has it that one company offering Jew Gold seeds under the name Kosher Kush had the mother plant blessed by a rabbi to make it Kosher… but, I find that extremely difficult to believe and will only entertain such bullshit if the rabbi himself tells me the story.*

joint- *n.* a cannabis cigarette… ugh, it is disgusting to use those two words in the same sentence unless it is: *After smoking more than a pack a day for eighteen years, medical cannabis helped me quit smoking cigarettes*; you can do it, too, you know… get verified and quit that devilweed that's causing cancer and smoke the God bud that's curing it; also, *joint* is a place where many innocent people are rotting due to ignorant and unjust cannabis prohibition laws

jonesing- *v.* to be fiending or in dire need of a cannabis fix; *see fix (no, really, see fix; you gotta see fix because it's all about the fix and you need a fix, don't you, 'cause I need a fix, so see fix and stop jonesing already)*

Juanita (juanita)- *n.* a colloquialism used for cannabis as a Latin allusion to the *Jane* in *Mary Jane*; *see marijuana, Mary Jane*

juice- *n.* the raw liquids expressed from fresh cannabis plant parts; the elixir of life; the fountain of youth; so much better tasting, almost palatable even, with a little lemon and a lot of honey or agave; —*v.* to *juice* raw cannabis

kaia- *n. see kaya*

kaneh bosom (kneh bosom)- *n. fragrant cane*; the biblical Hebrew term for cannabis, according to religious historian Sula Benet/Sara Benetowa, that appears five times in the Bible; most notably, *kaneh bosom* is in the recipe for the original anointing oil used by Jesus, his disciples, and countless servants of God; *see anointing oil, cannabis*

Kashmir- *n.* the northwestern region of South Asia, including portions of India, Pakistan and China; *archaic for Cashmere;* — *n. Kashmir (Cashmere)* indica landrace cannabis from this area; also, a Led Zeppelin song that is really trippy when you're fucked up on some *Kashmir*

kaya (kaia)- *n.* colloquial for cannabis as popularized by the eponymous Bob Marley song, *Kaya*, released in 1976

KB- *abbrv. see killer bud, kind*

kelp- *n.* seaweed such as Ascophyllum *nodosum* or Luminaria *digitata;* one of the singularly most useful organic amendments in the cannabis garden

key- *n.* colloquial for a kilo; *see kilo*

KGB- *abbrv. see killer green bud*

kief (kif, keef)- *n.* a specific type of cannabis concentrate comprised of the loose glandular trichome heads that have been knocked free from cannabis flowers through the use of force and typically a screen; there are numerous different classifications of kief worldwide, notably double *0* powder and sand

killer- *adj.* having the quality of excellent cannabis

killer bud- *n. see killer green bud*; an oxymoron, given that cannabis is actually *savior bud*

killer green bud- *n.* high quality sensimillia indoor cannabis

killing a skunk- *phr.* the description applied by survivalists and rednecks to smoking cannabis, and, occasionally, the preparation of the munchies to follow

kilo (kilogram)- *n.* a unit of measurement equivalent to two and two-tenths pounds that is often used to enumerate the quantity of cannabis seized in international raids

kind (the kind, kind bud, kind green bud)- *n.* cannabis of exceptional quality; usually, better than *killer bud*; often, *kind* is used with the article *the* for emphasis; *i.e. Boi, that girl always be growin' the kind!; —adj.* having the characteristic of *the kind*

king size- *adj.* having the characteristic of a joint that is approximately one hundred and ten millimeters long

kit- *n.* a small collection of cannabis flowers or concentrates, a smoking or vaping device, and some form of heat or combustion; usually, a *kit* is for one person or a small group of people who need to use cannabis during travel; occasionally, dabbers will refer to their tackle box as a *kit; for differentiation, see traveler, tackle box*

knife- *n.* the blade on which, or from which, one hot knifes or stabs a dab; *see hot knife, stab*

Krohn, Christopher- *n.* the heroic and legendary mayor of Santa Cruz, California, who stood proudly with WAMM in defiance of the federal government and their archaic, Draconian laws; *Krohn* is known for publicly administering medical cannabis to terminally ill patients on the steps of Santa Cruz City Hall immediately following the DEA raid of WAMM's medical cannabis garden; *see WAMM*

krumz (krums)- *n. see crumz*

112

kryptonite- *n.* colloquial for extremely potent cannabis, presumably because it could take down Superman; allow me to assure you that I am doing just fine, and still able to do all the shit I used to while high… just check the skies… you'll see me again there soon

Kryptonite- *n.* an indica dominant cannabis strain bred by Oaksterdam that is *Killer Queen x The Purps*

L (l)- *abbrv. see L-plate*

lab- *n. see cannabis lab;* also, *lab* can refer to the concentrate-making house that just exploded, because the extract artist needed a cig while blasting buds

lab testing- *v. see cannabis lab testing*

laced- *adj.* compromised with an additive; the deadly condition of all street cannabis that makes it so dangerous and lethal, according to your parents anyway; although never seen nor experienced by anyone I know, *laced* cannabis is supposedly cannabis leaf material saturated in cheap, dangerous synthetic drugs; bullshit; the only *laced* cannabis on the market are buds that have been soda popped; *see soda popping*

lack of motivation- *n.* one of the numerous fallacious side effects of cannabis use; honestly, if one has a *lack of motivation* while high, then she probably is unmotivated while drunk, or while on prescription narcotics, or while breathing; *i.e. How can you possibly say that one who consumes cannabis is guilty of having a lack of motivation when this heavy bud smoker literally wrote the book on cannabis in less than a month?*

ladies and gentlemen- *n.pl.* collectively, one's cannabis garden as it refers to all the ladies (female cannabis plants) and gentlemen (illegal immigrant workers) therein

Ladybud.- *n.* a women's lifestyle magazine centered primarily on cannabis

Lambsbread (Lambsbreath, Lamb's Bread)- *n.* a Jamaican sativa cannabis landrace; *Lambsbread* was supposedly Bob Marley's favorite strain

lamp- *n.* the glass dome or orb that is electrified in order to produce light in horticultural applications; for the record, as common wisdom suggests, a bulb grows and a *lamp* glows

landrace (landrace cannabis, cannabis landrace)- *n.* a variety or strain of cannabis endogenous to a specific geographical region that is typically from ancient origins; *i.e. There are numerous heirloom cannabis strains that have been bred from Afghani or Thai landrace cannabis varieties.*

Laos- *n.* a Laotian cannabis sativa landrace

larf- *n.* the ridiculous and ludicrous colloquial term for cannabis leaf, presumably originating from a douchebag millennial hipster or cannabis clown's misspelled text or tweet

larfy- *adj.* full of larf; leafy or airy as opposed to dense and chunky; *i.e. That green gold is pretty larfy... maybe we should name it Green Aluminum or Effin Rod.;* see leafy, larf

leach- *v. see flush*

leaf- *n.* a part of the cannabis anatomy, typically compound palmate (*see Ducksfoot for differentiation*); not the smokable part of the plant, but is a colloquial term for smokable cannabis; *leaf* is used most often in lower grade edibles and concentrates

Leafly- *n.* a cannabis website designed to help weed punks (or cannanewbies) find dispensaries, sort of learn (often inaccurate or incomplete) information about cannabis, and browse page after page of nice pastel pretty colors and fun bubbly lettering like one would expect from a pediatrician's website; *Leafly* is Weedmaps' main competition, but with more *information;* it seems to be targeted towards the twelve to twenty-year-old audience as opposed to the twenty-one and over crowd

leaf mold- *n.* decomposed and composted leaf remains from deciduous trees and shrubs that are high in nitrogen and microbiological activity and are often employed in the organic or biodynamic cannabis garden

leafy- *adj.* having the characteristic of cannabis flowers that are full of leaf instead of with flowers or buds; often, *leafy* is used synonymously with airy; a cannabis flower can become *leafy* for a number of reasons including low intensity light, poor quality soil or nutrient solution, or an excess of nitrogen during the flowering cycle

LEAP- *acronym* Law Enforcement Against Prohibition; thank you, officers, we greatly appreciate you being reasonable and supportive

LED- *abbrv.* light emitting diode, a type of lighting that has been adopted for horticultural applications; due to the light intensity versus heat output versus electricity usage of *LEDs,* they are an excellent choice for cultivating cannabis indoors; *i.e. You gotta get eye protection when running LED lights so you don't burn 'em outta your skull!*; anecdotally, it has been noticed that some cannabis plants do not stretch into flowering with *LED* lights like they do with all others, and this should be taken into consideration when deciding when to flip the light cycle to twelve-twelve

Lee, Martin A.- *n.* a cannabis author and activist responsible for creating Project CBD, and known for his books, *Acid Dreams: The Complete Social History of LSD: The CIA, the Sixties, and Beyond* and *Smoke Signals: A Social History of Marijuana- Medical, Recreational and Scientific; see Project CBD*

legal states- *n.pl.* any (or all) of the states in the US that has legalized cannabis for medical or recreational use; as of now, there are twenty-three states (Alaska, Arizona, California, Colorado, Connecticut, Delaware, Hawaii, Illinois, Maine, Maryland, Massachusetts, Michigan, Minnesota, Montana, Nevada, New Hampshire, New Jersey, New Mexico, New York, Oregon, Rhode Island, Vermont, and Washington) and Washington DC that have legalized medical or recreational cannabis; states that have passed CBD-only laws do not qualify as *legal states…* how can a sovereignty criminalize a strawberry but legalize the vitamin C inside?

legalization- *n.* the act of making cannabis legal with exceptions instead of fully decriminalized; *i.e. The vast majority of cannabis legislation presented to the California public for 2016 is legalization-centered, not decriminalization-centered, which inherently makes them illogical and thinly veiled instruments of prohibition. Ah, the irony.; for differentiation, see decriminalization*

legalize it- *phr.* the economical battle cry of the contemporary terrorist army composed of pacifists and narcissists who are fueled into cultural carnage by the evil mind-control drug known as power-in-the-name-of-cannabis; the mantra of our modern social jihad; literally, *legalize it* means *make cannabis legal worldwide*

Lemon Skunk- *n.* a sativa dominant cannabis strain popularized by Green House Seed Co. and DNA Genetics that is *Skunk #1 x Citral*; the original cut is from Las Vegas, Nevada, and is about the only good thing to ever come out of such a damned place; a particular characteristic of *Lemon Skunk* is that she works exponentially better on inflammation than most strains, likely due to significant levels of CBG and CBD present with the THC

lettuce- *n. see devil weed*

lid- *n.* an old school unit of measurement used prior to the more universal implementation of the metric weights and measures; according to several old-timers, a *lid* referred to the amount of cannabis that could be placed on the top of one tobacco can lid, or about four-finger's worth (measured like one measures liquor); often, when this term is used, people assume that a *lid* is one ounce of cannabis; *i.e. For my wedding, I smoked a whole lid of green rolled in a Cheech 'n' Chong Big Bambú album paper and was lit as... uh, what were we talking about? Who are you? Where the fuck am I? I'm married?*

lifted- *adj.* high, as in *lifted* up on high

light deprivation (light dep)- *n.* a cannabis cultivation practice where the number of growing or lighted hours is manually reduced, usually using tarps or covers, in order to induce or initiate flowering; —*light dep adj.* having the characteristic of outdoor or greenhouse cannabis that has been forced to flower off-season through *light deprivation; i.e. Since there is an abundance of intense light in the summer, her light dep flowers are ginormous!*

light emitting plasma (light emitting plasma fixture)- *n.* a specific type of advancement in horticultural lighting that offers an intense range of light spectrum closely resembling that of the sun; invented by Tesla

light up (light it up)- *v.* to ignite cannabis for the purpose of consuming the smoke; *i.e. She likes to light up before mass in order to stomach the misogynistic sermon and the hypocritical alcoholic assholes sitting next to her.*

lighter- *n.* a device that is filled with fuel, topped with a flint, and used to ignite a flame or wick for combusting cannabis or cannabis concentrates; if one is to smoke cannabis instead of vape it, one must adhere to this practical wisdom: the higher quality butane *lighter* used, the safer, smoother and tastier the smoke; note that I say butane *lighter,* not one of the refillable metal ones that make 1950s cigarette smokers look so damn cool and that use fuels that are unsafe to inhale; this is one of my main complaints about the continuity editors and the writers of numerous Hollywood films; too many movies have cannabis smokers using refillable *lighters*, which demonstrates a grave lack of authenticity; no, you're not gangsta or down or the shit if you use one of these lighters to smoke cannabis, you're just fucking stupid

lime- *n.* an alkaline derivative of limestone composed of calcium oxide that is used in cannabis cultivation as a soil or medium buffer

limonene- *n.* a common terpene found in cannabis that has a citrus, turpentine aroma; as it is one of the primary medical constituents of citrus, *limonene* has undergone numerous scientific studies that have determined its efficacy as a chemopreventative; *limonene* is further proof that cannabis is indeed an invaluable medicine

linalool- *n.* a common terpene found in cannabis that has a spicy floral aroma; as it is one of the primary medical constituents of basil and other healing herbs, *linalool* has undergone numerous scientific studies that have determined its efficacy as a sedative and stress reliever; *linalool* is further proof that cannabis is indeed an invaluable medicine

liquid chromatography (high performance liquid chromatography, HPLC)- *n.* a chemistry technique used to analyze, identify, or quantify the chemical composition of a laboratory sample; since it is far more accurate than gas chromatography, cannabis testing facilities often use high performance *liquid chromatography* to test the potency of a cannabis sample; *for differentiation, see gas chromatography, spectroscopy*

lit (lit up)- *adj. see high; i.e. I'm lit as fuck, writing a dictionary, and couldn't be happier.*

live resin- *n.* a solvent-extracted cannabis concentrate created by running fresh, uncured, wet cannabis flowers with butane or another solvent; the presence of multiple facings of various types of *live resin* is likely evidence that an unscrupulous dispensary owner or provider is blasting buds in order to double his profits; *i.e. For the obvious reason, I am suspicious of the flowers at farmacies that sell a lot of live resin.*

load- *v.* to pack or fill a bowl or oven with cannabis prior to consumption; —*n.* the amount of cannabis placed in a bowl or oven

loaded- *adj.* the state of being filled with cannabis for consumption as in a packed bowl or oven; also, *loaded* refers to one's state of being that is as full of cannabis as a *loaded* bowl is; *i.e. Did you load the bowl? 'Yeah, it's loaded.' Great, cuz I wanna get loaded.*

loaded potato- *n.* a couch potato who is stoned; *i.e. Since I don't have starch for brains, I dislike becoming a loaded potato after smoking a super heavy indica.*

loam- *n.* a soil or soil mix that has roughly equal parts of evenly distributed humus, sand or other rock aerator, and clay; —*loamy adj.* having the quality or characteristic of loam; *i.e. Cannabis prefers to grow in a nutrient rich loamy soil comprised of ingredients like compost, perlite, vermiculite, pumice, leaf mold, worm castings, and other organic amendments.*

lock out (lock-out)- *n. see nutrient lock out*

locoweed- *n.* a derogatory colloquialism for cannabis based on the effects the real locoweed Oxytropis or Datura have on livestock and humans, respectively

lost- *adj.* an oxymoronic colloquialism for feeling the effects of cannabis consumption; in fact, cannabis can lead to getting *lost*, if one so desires, but is more guilty of allowing a person to be *found...* either metaphysically or by the authorities

loud- *adj.* yet another brilliant classic from the infantile minds of weed nerds that is a colloquial term used to signify cannabis with such a strong odor that it collapses the sense time continuum in order to be heard; *i.e. The budtender was talking about how loud this strain is over how loud that strain is, and I just be sittin' there like: "Cannabis has an odor that smells not sounds.... Can you taste what I'm sayin', dipshit?"*

Love Genetics- *n.* an innovative, boutique, medical cannabis genetics organization with the belief that cannabinoids and terpenes work together synergistically; *Love Genetics* aims to infuse high THC strains with high levels of CBD, create strains with outrageous terpenes, and develop unique hybrids from extremely rare genetics

low sperm count- *n.* one of the terrifying rumored side effects of cannabis use; a study reported by a clearly anti-cannabis *scientific* publication claims that cannabis use causes a *low sperm count* in males who use frequently; the cited study was of a small sample of fewer than two thousand men all from a very specific geographical region and did not fully take into consideration environmental factors or accurately control for alcohol, caffeine or tobacco use; as evidence in contrary to the *low sperm count* hypothesis, I offer my entire generation who was birthed to pot-smoking hippies

low temp- *v. see flavorbomb*

***L*-plate (*L, l, l-plate*)-** *n.* a specific type of hand-rolled cone that is made by gluing together two rolling papers in an *L* shape; often, but not always, an *L-plate* has cannabis mixed together with tobacco and employs the use of a crutch

Luminary Beacon, Luminary Profiler- *n.* a lab-grade instrument developed by Sage Analytics that uses spectroscopy to test cannabis samples for potency in the privacy of one's own home or dispensary without destroying the sample material; there are numerous benefits to the *Luminary Beacon*, including sample preservation, immediate results, and the ability to inexpensively batch test; *i.e. I cannot wait until I can afford to run a Luminary Beacon in my CBD garden.*

Mac (Macintosh, Mac Tabby)- *n.* the name given to any cat who loves cannabis, derived from Macintosh Tabby, The Kashmir Cat, a famous tabby known for his insatiable medical cannabis consumption (he has a bad back); *i.e. That Mac cat loves to get blazed and watch MØ videos with me.*

macronutrients- *n.pl.* the major nutrients required for growth by all plants

macros- *abbrv. see macronutrients*

magar (cannagar)- *n.* a cannabis cigar rolled with ground cannabis flowers in a cannabis leaf (or leaves) instead of with tobacco; literally, *magar* is a conjunction of *marijuana* and *cigar*; the term has since been adopted by a company for their high-end and rather pricey cannabis cigars

magic brownie- *n.* a culinary delight composed of ground cannabis flowers, cannabis-infused oil, or cannabis butter, and brownie making ingredients; occasionally in the past, a *magic brownie* also contained additional seasoning from the psilocybin mushroom spice jar

magnesium sulfate (Epsom salt)- *n.* a mineral compound used in cannabis cultivation to assist the plant in the production of chlorophyll, make available other nutrients, or flush the medium of excess salt buildup; *see flushing solution*

magnetic ballast- *n. see ballast*

mahjoun- *n.* a heavily spiced Moroccan hash jam that is similar to majoun; *for disambiguation, see majoun*

majoun- *n.* a traditional Moroccan confection usually made with a cannabis and honey paste that can include walnuts, dates, raisins, figs, ginger, anise, cardamom, hempseed, sesame seed, nutmeg, turmeric, cashews or poppy seed; *majoun* means *love potion* in Arabic; *i.e. Majoun: it's not your grandma's* *fruitcake… or maybe it is, if you're lucky!;* my recipe for *majoun* is:

Mad June **Majoun**

½ cup ground organic roasted and salted cashews or shelled pistachios

¼ cup organic hulled hempseed

1 tbsp. organic white sesame seed

1 tsp. organic fennel seed

¼ ounce ground dried top-shelf cannabis flowers (approx. 10 grams before the stems are removed)

2 tbsp. organic red palm oil

1 tbsp. organic virgin coconut oil

1 tsp. finely chopped fresh or crystalized organic ginger

1 tsp. organic cardamom or ginger powder

¼ cup minced organic sweetened dried tart cherries, like Montmorency

¼ cup chopped organic dried pineapple

¼ cup organic light agave

5 grams decarboxylated kief, rosin, CO2 oil, or bubble hash

for rolling:

¼ cup organic unsweetened shredded coconut

¼ cup organic hulled hempseed

1 tbsp. organic coconut palm sugar

½-1 gram decarboxylated kief

In a shallow, dry frying pan, slowly toast nuts, hempseed, sesame seed, fennel seed, and ground cannabis over medium heat for five minutes, stirring frequently to prevent scorching. Add red palm oil, coconut oil and chopped ginger, mix together, and sauté over very low heat for another seven minutes, stirring often. Add cardamom or ginger powder, cherries, pineapple, and agave syrup, then toss to coat. Sauté this over low heat for another five minutes, stirring as needed to prevent sugars from burning. Remove *majoun* mixture from heat and cool slowly until it can be held comfortably, approximately ten to thirty minutes. With gloved hands, thoroughly work decarboxylated kief or concentrate into the seed and fruit mix and form into thirteen small balls or squares, or seven larger-dose balls. Or, shape into a log to slice off individually sized portions as desired. Then, roll or coat the *majoun* in the coconut, hempseed, coconut palm sugar, and kief, and let set on parchment paper or a silicone mat. Package and store or serve the *majoun* as needed. Depending on the potency of the input material, each small confection is approximately 250 to 1000 milligrams of total active cannabinoids (so use caution and do not provide to cannanewbies).

Malawi (Malawi Gold, Chamba)- *n.* a sativa cannabis landrace from Malawi, Africa; considered to be one of the highest quality cannabis varieties in the world; estimates place *Malawi* as one of the three most lucrative exports from Malawi, along with tilapia and tea

mango- *n.* the fruit, Mangifera *indica,* that has extremely elevated levels of the terpene myrcene and is purported to enhance the effects of lower quality smokable cannabis in a similar manner as ginger and black pepper; *see ginger, black pepper, myrcene, terpenes*

manicure- *v.* to carefully cut and remove the remnants of leaf material and trim from around a cannabis flower as one of the last steps prior to curing; strictly speaking, *manicuring* is the meticulous fine trimming of ripe and dried cannabis flowers; *for differentiation, see trim*

marihuana- *n. see marijuana, cannabis*

marijuana (marihuana)- *n.* a Hispanic term for smokable cannabis as opposed to the derivatives and extracts of the drug that were being commonly used in medicines at the time of the introduction of the word into our US language and culture; a derogatory term for cannabis founded in racism; during the 1930s, newly elected dictator of the infant Federal Bureau of Narcotics, Harry Anslinger, is noted for saying: "Marijuana is the most violence-causing drug in the history of mankind... Most marijuana smokers are Negroes, Hispanics, Filipinos and entertainers. Their satanic music, jazz and swing, result from marijuana usage"; this statement, and the riotous racist furor it precipitated, ultimately led to the criminalization of cannabis in the United States and the world; we all know the US is founded on bigotry, but did you ever think it went so deep as to have prevented the world's civilizations from having legal access to such a powerful medicine and nutritious food source?

marijuana refugees (cannabis refugees)- *n.pl.* patients and families of patients who emigrate from intolerant unions to medical cannabis havens like California and Colorado in order to legally procure their life-saving medicine

marinate- *v.* to smoke or vape cannabis, especially to hotbox or clambake and then soak in the ambient smoke known as the marinade; —*marinade n.* the smoke that fills a hotboxed room; *i.e. Enchantress smoke is my favorite marinade… it just lingers in the air like a berry, grape and kush air freshener. Maybe someday you can marinate with her, too.; —marinated adj.* having the quality or characteristic of having soaked in a marinade; also, extremely high, to the point of being saturated

Marinol- *n.* a dangerous, FDA-approved, synthetic cannabinoid drug that has a significantly lower medical efficacy than that of whole-plant cannabis flower or whole-plant cannabis concentrate and has a much higher instance and occurrence of negative side effects; further proof in the argument for nationwide, whole-plant, medical cannabis legalization legislation

Marley, Bob- *n.* a Rastafarian reggae and cannabis legend known for singing political and community songs and supporting the use of cannabis for spiritual and recreational purposes; recently, the estate of *Bob Marley* has allowed his name to be used on cannabis products for sale

Mary Jane- *n.* a colloquialism for cannabis that is used as an obvious allusion to the term *marijuana*

Maui Wowie- *n.* an unknown sativa dominant heirloom cannabis strain from Hawaii that was popularized in the 1960s; *Maui Wowie* is not to be confused with a blowjob on the Maui sands at sunset from a Polynesian hula dancer

Measure 2- *n.* the legislation in Alaska that legalized cannabis for adult recreational use; but, alas(ka), no one cared

Measure 91- *n.* the legislation in Oregon that legalized cannabis for adult recreational use

medible (edible)- *n.* a medicated edible; a cannabis-infused consumable; *medibles* are not recommended for novices, as they typically contain between fifty to one thousand milligrams of THC per item, and the standard daily dose of THC is ten to fifty milligrams; *medibles* are not a legitimate way to consume medical cannabis... if you believe otherwise, just ask for your next antibiotic or other pharmaceutical prescription to be administered in a brownie or cookie and see what the pharmacist says

medical cannabis- *n.* cannabis or a cannabis derived medical preparation prescribed or recommended by a licensed physician that is intended for human consumption and used for the treatment of any disease or medical condition, or for any healing purpose, including but not limited to the treatment, prevention, or relief of acid reflux, acne, ADD/ADHD, addiction, AIDS, ALS, Alzheimer's, anorexia, antibiotic resistance, anxiety, atherosclerosis, arthritis, asthma, autism, bigotry, bipolar disorder, degenerative bone diseases, bronchitis, cancer, chronic pain, colitis/Crohn's, depression, diabetes, eating disorders, endocrine disorders, epilepsy/seizures, fibromyalgia, gastrointestinal disorders, glaucoma, heart disease, Huntington's, infections, inflammation, injury, irritable bowel syndrome, kidney disease, liver disease, metabolic syndrome, migraines, mood disorders, motion sickness, multiple sclerosis, nausea, neurodegeneration, neuropathic pain, obesity, OCD, osteoporosis, Parkinson's, Prion/Mad Cow disease, PTSD, rheumatism, schizophrenia, sickle cell anemia, skin conditions, sleep disorders, spinal cord injury, stress, stroke/TBI, weight loss, or vertigo

medically endorsed marijuana stores- *n.pl.* the name given to recreational cannabis stores in Washington State that are now allowed to legally tax and gouge medical cannabis patients, because the recreational store owners couldn't figure out how to survive with competition in a capitalist market (so, they fucking whined to the politicians to get the law changed)

medicate- *v.* to use cannabis for medical purposes; *for differentiation, see poser, reformer*

medicine- *n. see meds*

medium- *n.* the soil, soilless mix, or other substrate used for cannabis cultivation as the functional substance in which the roots can flourish and support the weight of the plant

meds- *abbrv.* medical cannabis; medical cannabis is *medicine, not fyah tree, dawg; i.e. Please do not ever refer to my meds as fire, tree, loud, larfy or amazon, or by any reference or euphemism that relates to dangerous and addictive drugs like liquid cocaine, crack, vodka, LSD, or strawberry daiquiris. Your compliance is appreciated and required, thank you.*

mellow- *adj. see chill*

mellow fellow- *n.* a term of endearment for an older man who smokes or consumes a great deal of cannabis; *i.e. It'd be a trip if my dad was a mellow fellow… maybe he is and I don't even know.*

melt- *v.* to lose integrity and become liquid prior to vaporization, as in the heating of a quality cannabis rosin

memory loss- *n.* one of the numerous fallacious side effects of cannabis use; in fact, low-dose high THC cannabis has been shown to prevent and reverse the effects of dementia and

Alzheimer's in patients; *i.e. I've smoked a bunch of cannabis in my life, and I have never experienced memory loss from it… just memory misplacement.*

mendo- *n.* colloquial for strong, indica dominant cannabis that usually originates in Mendocino County, CA; not to be confused with *menudo*, which is a Hispanic food many people scarf down after smoking some *mendo*

Mendocino County- *n.* the storied location of some of the world's greatest outdoor cannabis cultivation; *Mendocino County* is partially responsible for supplying the entire US with the majority of its cannabis; *for differentiation, see Emerald Triangle, Humboldt County, Trinity County*

Mendo Purps- *n.* an indica cannabis strain from Northern California that is said to be a backcross of a North American landrace indica; rumor has it that *Mendo Purps* and *Granddaddy Purple* are the same strain, or are nearly genetically identical; having grown both in the same room at the same time, I can say that they may share common ancestry, but they are definitely not the same phenotype of the same strain

menthol- *n.* a common terpene found in cannabis that has a sharp mint aroma; as it is one of the primary medical constituents of peppermint and other mints, *menthol* has undergone numerous scientific studies that have determined its efficacy as an anti-irritant and localized anesthetic; *menthol* is further proof that cannabis is indeed an invaluable medicine

metabolic shift (metabolic growth shift, metabolism transition)- *n.* the major changes in maturation and metabolism that cannabis undergoes during its life cycle; these periods of *metabolic shift* vary in duration and occur usually at the following times: seed to seedling, seedling to teen; teen to full vegetative growth; growth to flower formation; flower formation to seed production (if pollinated) or flower ripening

128

metal halide (MH, metal halide lamp)- *n.* a specific type of HID horticultural lighting heavy in the blue spectrum of light that is most commonly used during the vegetative cycle of cannabis growth; LEDs are quickly replacing *metal halide lamps* as the industry standard for the vegetative cycle of cannabis growth

me, too- *phr.* the description given to cannabis products or strains that are exactly the same as another company's or organization's; the *me, too* phenomenon appears to be most prevalent in the cannabis breeding game, where it seems every breeder has exactly the same strains as every other breeder (and the occasional house line comprised of unknowns)… how many of them all have OG Kush, Sour Diesel, Headband, Fire OG, Girl Scout Cookies…?; *i.e. I find most breeders and breeding companies to be rather boring. They are full of a bunch of me, too strains that everyone can get at any dispensary in clone form or seed form from any other breeder… why wouldn't they want to be different and unique, and why wouldn't they actually want to breed something for themselves? Oh, right: they don't have any fucking skills, or they don't think doing it the right fuckin' way will make them as much money.*

Mexican (Oaxaca Sativa)- *n.* a cannabis landrace sativa from Mexico

Mexican brick bud (redbud, dirtweed)- *n.* poor quality, seeded female and male cannabis plants that were harvested whole and pressed together in large bales from which *bricks* were cut off for sale after export across the border; Proposition 215 in California has virtually eliminated the influx of brick bud from Mexico; in the novel of the life of cannabis, *Mexican brick bud* is the foil to California greenbud

MH- *abbrv. see metal halide*

micos- *abbrv. see mycorrhizae*

microbiologicals- *n.pl.* the group of beneficial microorganisms used in cannabis cultivation to aid in the absorption of nutrients, the decomposition of dead roots, and the protection against soil pathogens or diseases; *microbiologicals* are to cannabis as probiotics are to humans; beneficial bacteria and mycorrhizae are specific types of *microbiologicals*

micron- *n.* one millionth of a meter; the unit of measurement used to differentiate grades of hash or kief based on the size of the screen being employed in the extraction process; common *micron* sizes for hash making are 38, 45, 73, 90, 110, 160, and 220; μ is the symbol designating *microns*; unfortunately, due to the ignorance and complicit complacency when education is required that is rampant among cannabis clowns, a differentiation is necessary: the word is *micron*, not *millimeter...* say it with me, *micron*

micronutrients- *n.pl.* all the secondary nutrients required for growth by plants

micros- *abbrv. see micronutrients*

midgrade (mid grade)- *n.* the category or shelf that can be classified by having the extraordinary and astounding characteristic of mediocrity; *midgrade* is the middle-priced, middle-quality cannabis of a specific dispensary; —*adj.* having the quality or cost of the *midgrade*

midrange meds (midgrade meds, mid range buds)- *n.pl. see midgrade*

Mike O'Righzee- *n.* your Irish friend who bugs you and is a *fun guy*

Milagro Oil- *n.* the food-grade full extract cannabis oil used by WAMM to treat patients with severe or terminal illness like cancer

Miron glass- *n. see violetglass*

miticides- *n.pl.* the collective group of pesticides specifically designed for prevention or destruction of spider mites that have infested or can infest cannabis plants; *miticides* are not to be confused with the crablouse spray Mary Jane Watson uses to rid herself of *spidey mites*

Miyagi- *n.* colloquial for wax, as if there could ever be a comparison to one of wisdom and one who dabs; *i.e. Most people who call wax Miyagi weren't even born when the original movie came out.*

MJ- *abbrv. see Mary Jane*

Moby Dick- *n.* a sativa dominant cannabis strain bred by Dinafem that is a cross of *White Widow* and an undisclosed *Haze;* I include this strain to demonstrate that some cannabis people are in fact literary; what would truly demonstrate a sense of humor is if they called a *Moby Dick* hybrid *Ishmael*

molasses- *n.* the viscous, dark and sweet byproduct of sugar manufacture that is often used in cannabis cultivation due to its high potassium and carbohydrate concentrations; *see carbohydrates*

moldy- *adj.* full of mold; any cannabis that is *moldy* must be immediately discarded as it is a health hazard to humans

Moms for Marijuana- *n.* a pro-cannabis activist group founded by Serra Frank and now run (into a cliff) by Cheryl Shuman, the self-proclaimed *Martha Stewart of Pot*; though, given the illustrious incarcerated past of Ms. Stewart, it may not be wise for Ms. Shuman to draw such comparisons for the universe may view it as a line in the sand

mondo chrondo- *n.* a juvenile colloquialism for cannabis

moon rocks- *n.pl.* the name given to caviar by rapper Kurupt that is now commonly considered to be of higher quality than caviar due to the base materials supposedly being from the connoisseur shelf

mosquito preventing bits or granules- *n.pl. see Bacillus thuringiensis*

mota- *n.* a Latin American word used colloquially for cannabis; *i.e. I'd rather mota boat a hottie than motorboat her.*

mota boat- *v.* ostensibly, to motorboat your girl's titties while exhaling a large hit of cannabis smoke or vapor

mother- *n.* a female cannabis plant that has been kept in a vegetative stasis in order to produce a near endless supply of cuttings for cloning; —*v.* to keep a *mother* cannabis plant

mothering- *v. see mother*

mother room- *n.* an indoor cultivation room designed specifically to keep cannabis mothers in a productive stasis under a minimum of eighteen hours of light

mowing the lawn- *phr. see cutting the grass*

MPP- *abbrv.* the Marijuana Policy Project; an impotent organization that serves to influence politics through the powerful financial use of the social tool known as lobbying

mulch- *n.* a layer of organic material spread around the base of a cannabis plant in order to prevent premature evaporation of precious water; —*v.* to spread a layer of *mulch*

mull- *n.* a colloquialism for cannabis, especially cannabis that has been ground; often, *mull* is the term used to describe a mix of ground cannabis and tobacco; —*v.* to grind cannabis

munchies (the munchies)- *n.* the ferocious hunger often associated with the use of cannabis in general, but is actually only a side effect from certain cannabis strains rich in terpineol, myrcene, CBN and/or THC; also, *munchies* are the food that is consumed when one has *the munchies; —munchie adj.* having the quality of the cannabis that produces *the munchies; i.e. Fuck, that Sunset Sherbet sure is munchie.*

mushroom compost- *n.* a specific type of compost made from the spent remains of mushroom cultivation mediums or substrates; *mushroom compost* is often more basic than other types of compost and is occasionally used in cannabis cultivation where compost is needed but the soil is too acidic for application of garden compost; in conjunction with the other types of compost and worm castings, adding *mushroom compost* makes for a more complete compost composition and the richest possible environment for cannabis roots

mycorrhizae- *n.pl.* beneficial fungi that form a symbiotic relationship with plant roots and allow for nutrient absorption by the plant; there are two main types of *mycorrhizae*: endo and ecto; *mycorrhizae* are one of several beneficial organisms classified as microbiologicals that aid cannabis in its growth; *see microbiologicals*

mykos- *n.pl. see mycorrhizae*

myrcene- *n.* a common terpene found in cannabis that has a herbal floral aroma; as it is one of the primary medical constituents of mangoes, lemongrass, bay, hops and ylang-ylang, *myrcene* has undergone numerous scientific studies that have determined its efficacy as an anti-inflammatory, antibiotic, analgesic sedative; *myrcene* is further proof that cannabis is indeed an invaluable medicine

Nag Champa- *n.* the omnipresent incense used by stoners, college students and bohippians to mask the odor of cannabis that at once becomes an olfactory siren announcing the presence of cannabis smoking

nail- *n.* in the coffin of dabbers; the t-shaped device placed in the slide of a bong or dab rig that is heated to the point of glowing and then has a dab or glob of concentrate placed on the top to be vaporized and inhaled immediately

naphtha- *n.* a poisonous solvent; flammable liquid hydrocarbon distillation of petroleum; one should not consume any extract of cannabis that has been made using *naphtha*; it is an ingredient in camp fuel and is highly dangerous; the residue has been known to cause death, cancer and other serious illnesses that cannabis is meant to cure

naturalized- *adj.* made to be indigenous to an area over time through natural propagation in an uncultivated area; *naturalized* cannabis is a strain or variety that has been allowed to breed wild in an area, but was not originally from that area like a landrace would be; *for differentiation, see landrace*

nectar- *n.* pretentious for honey oil; more specifically, *nectar* is honey oil extracted from fresh or fresh-frozen cannabis flowers as opposed to cured buds or trim; typically, *nectar* contains more terpenes than other forms of solvent-extracted concentrates; *see honey oil*

needle- *n. see dab tool*

neem oil- *n.* oil from the seeds of the Azadirachta *indica*, or Indian Lilac, that is used as an all-natural, safe leaf shine and pesticide in cannabis cultivation

Nelson, Willie- *n.* a country folk singer and iconic cannabis advocate and legend; *Willie Nelson* is quite possibly the most commonly known public cannabis user and is at the center of much cannabis lore and legend; if one is to believe everything about Mr. Nelson, then he is a pothead hippie outlaw who can roll a joint in one hand in less than a minute at the same time as fully smoking an entire joint in one inhale while walking across the White House lawn hand in hand with a baked Bill Clinton; of course, this cannot be true given the sourpuss presence of Hillary… remember, you can never trust a woman who wears a pant suit, because she works for *the man*

Nepalese- *n.* a Himalayan indica cannabis landrace from Nepal; is it true that the higher the plant is grown, the higher the smoker gets?

nerolidol- *n.* a common terpene found in cannabis that has a fresh woody aroma; as it is one of the primary medical constituents of neroli, ginger, jasmine, and tea tree, *nerolidol* has undergone numerous scientific studies that have determined its efficacy as an antifungal and antimalarial sedative; *nerolidol* is further proof that cannabis is indeed an invaluable medicine

neutral- *adj.* having the quality of the state of being in balance in pH or inert in activity like that of water or a sterile soilless medium or amendment used in cannabis cultivation; *i.e. Vermiculite is a neutral soil conditioner, whereas cottonseed meal is an acidic amendment.*

Neville's Haze- *n. see Schoenmaker, Neville*

nice- *adj.* high or stoned; also, *nice* can be used to refer to having the characteristic of exceptional quality cannabis flowers or concentrates; —*nice (get nice) n.* exceptional cannabis flowers; *i.e. Let's score some get nice and, well, go get nice off that nice nice!*

nickel (nickel bag)- *n.* a small bag of cannabis containing five dollars worth of flowers; also, a *nickel* can be one-half gram of cannabis; a street dealer's slang, *nickel* is rapidly becoming archaic as more and more areas legalize cannabis and fewer people can divide buds into increments that small

ninja dab- *n.* the act of quickly and unsuspectingly sabotaging a person by adding an additional glob to the nail while he is inhaling the dab he already put there; the atrocious dabbing practice equivalent to that of some guy slipping a roofy into some chick's drink so he can (date) rape her later; I include *ninja dab* only to further illustrate that there may be some truth to the stereotype that dabbers are assholes... why else would they have the need for the term if they weren't?

ninja hermie- *n.* a male banana on a female cannabis plant that has remained hidden from daily examination, or quickly appeared during the last day or two of flowering prior to harvest; typically, *ninja hermies* are not a problem for the parent flower, but can pose a great risk for any remaining strains ripening in the garden; *i.e. Bud quality and profit drop exponentially if a ninja hermie pollinates the rest of the garden and creates thousands of tiny little immature seeds.; ninja hermie* is not to be confused with your Gemini friend who secretly has both a cock and a pussy

nitrogen- *n.* along with phosphorous and potassium, one of the three major elements used by cannabis plants for growth and development; *nitrogen* specifically aids in the production of chlorophyll and increases vegetative growth; although it is necessary through the entire life cycle, especially to feed the microbiologicals and prevent chlorosis, *nitrogen* should be reduced drastically during the flowering period

node- *n.* the point on the stem of a plant at which branching, leafing or flowering occur; *for differentiation, see internode, tri-nodality*

nonpsychoactive- *adj.* not psychoactive; *for differentiation, see psychoactive*

nonpsychoactive medical cannabis- *n.* the paltry consolation offered by states with lawmakers who have fallen victim to the grave disease known as Catholic guilt

NORML (Norml)- *acronym* the National Organization for the Reform of Marijuana Laws; *see Keith Stroup*

Northern Lights- *n.* an *Afghani* indica heirloom cannabis strain from the 1980s that single handedly changed the cannabis breeding industry worldwide; along with *Skunk #1* and *Haze*, *Northern Lights* is one of three strains found in the genetics of nearly every contemporary hybrid; *Northern Lights* could have been to what God was referring when she said, "Let there be light!"

NPK (N-P-K)- *abbrv.* nitrogen, phosphorous, potassium; the standardized listing of these elements required by law to be visible on the packaging of any fertilizer or nutrient designed for use on plants or in plant cultivation

nuggets (nuggetry)- *n.pl. see nugs*

nug porn- *n. see pot shots, High Times Magazine*

nug-run (nug run)- *adj.* having the quality of a cannabis concentrate created by running or blasting whole cannabis flowers as opposed to trim, shake or bottom buds

nugs- *n.pl.* dried cannabis flowers, so-called for their rock-like density in some cases; the gold selling *nugs* brings in

nute burn- *n.* the scorching of cannabis that has been overfed hydroponic nutrients or all-purpose fertilizers; *i.e. When I saw the nute burn on the cuttings I had given him, my heart broke... I felt really bad for the plants and that I gave them to someone so incapable and negligent.*

nutes- *n.pl.* hydroponic nutrients; many brands of *nutes* are plant and patient poisons and should never be used; *nutes* can be homemade and organic

nutrient deficiency- *n.* a condition of lacking one or more specific nutrients; most often, this is due to a lack of the nutrient, but occasionally *nutrient deficiency* can occur due to a pH imbalance in the medium that has caused nutrient lock out or chlorosis

nutrient film technique- *n.* a type of hydroponic cannabis cultivation where a thin layer of nutrient-rich solution is washed or bathed across the roots of cannabis plants and drained, and then allowed to dry for an allotted time before repeating the process several times a day

nutrient lock out- *n.* the condition of a cannabis medium that is extremely high or low in pH such that the plant cannot absorb nutrients necessary for life

nutrients- *n.pl.* the collective group of necessary elements and minerals absolutely required for all cannabis to successfully grow

nuts- *n.pl.* colloquial for cannabis seeds; *i.e. Hey, have you tried the beans from that new breeder, Deez Nuts, yet? Wonder what Snoop thinks of them all...*

Oaksterdam- *n.* the infamous *university* in Oakland, California, that was once dismantled by the federal government and has now reopened; after seeing much of the information being disseminated by the so-called experts teaching classes there, I must say that *Oaksterdam* needs to make *The Doobieous Dictionary* required reading for its students… and possibly its faculty members

Oaxacan- *n. see Mexican*

Obsidian Oil- *n.* a specific type of full extract cannabis oil popularized by Love Genetics that is made using only water, pressure and heat to fully extract all the potential medical benefits of whole-plant cannabis; despite common misconception, oil and alcohol-soluble cannabinoids and terpenes can be fully extracted using water; the process to make *Obsidian Oil* combines the mechanics of making bubble hash, the pressurized extraction of juices and absorbed liquids through a fine micron screen (like 38 or 73 μ, depending on the desired end product), and the act of temperature and time controlled simmering to separate the oils, fats, lipids, plant waxes and resins from the water; *Obsidian Oil* is decarboxylated in the process of simmering and is intended to be the safest method of making and ingesting full extract cannabis oil, but is not intended to be combusted or vaporized

odor- *n.* the smell of cannabis

odor control- *n.* the collective group of industrial items used to purify the air of an indoor cannabis grow op in order to scrub it clean of odors; these items include carbon filters, ozone generators, and aerosolized deodorizers; *see carbon filter, ozone generator, deodorizers*

OG Kush- *n.* a legendary indica dominant hybrid with mythical and supposedly unconfirmed origins; if one is to believe all the rumors, *OG Kush* is actually an Original Ocean Gangsta Grown hybrid of *Chemdawg-4, Hindu Kush, Ghost, Lemon Thai, Tahoe, Pakistani, Triangle Kush* and the motherfucking kitchen sink; the truth is, "OG" stands for ocean grown, and the rest is a clusterfuck of rumors and lies (and posers attempting to claim shit that isn't theirs), and the true origins supposedly remain unverified

oil- *n.* any liquid cannabis concentrate, especially one that is thick, dark amber and viscous as opposed to waxy or crumbly; *for differentiation, see cannabis-infused oil, full extract cannabis oil, honey oil, concentrates*

oiler- *n.* a cannabis joint rolled with flowers and a cannabis concentrate like oil or wax; a cannabis joint that has been coated in some fashion or another with a cannabis concentrate; *for differentiation, see reefer, tarantula*

oil press- *n.* a type of cannabis extractor that uses pressure and heat to forcibly exude or extract fresh resins from dried and cured cannabis flowers without the use of solvents, including water; *i.e. A hair straightener is used as a makeshift micro oil press for the production of rosin.*

oil rig (oil-rig)- *n. see dab rig*

Oldsog (Oldsog SSH)- *n.* a select cutting of the famous sativa, *Super Silver Haze*

OMRI- *abbrv.* Organic Materials Review Institute; the organization that reviews fertilizers and amendments and determines whether or not they meet the stringent requirements to qualify for use in certified organic cultivation; if at all possible, one should only use *OMRI* listed amendments and USDA Organic products for cannabis cultivation

one-hitter- *n.* a small, usually cylindrical or ovoid, straight smoking pipe with a bowl that holds the approximate amount of cannabis equal to one hit; *one-hitters* are frequently used as travel or road pipes due to their similarity in size, shape and smoking style to a tobacco cigarette; *i.e. He pulled over at a rest* *stop on his way to Perris and toked up a one-hitter before headin' on down the line.*

one-hit-wonder (one hit wonder)- *n.* a derogatory phrase for a person who can only consume one hit of cannabis before they are WOOOOOOO!; a term for cannabis so strong that it only takes one hit to get high; a biological impossibility for some people; *i.e. They call Gorilla Glue #4 one-hit-wonder shit, but I just smoked an eighth of it to my head and I can st illtyp equitefine...*

one love- *phr.* the former mantra of the cannabis community originating from a Bob Marley song that was once used to describe the thread of love for cannabis and each other that connected all cannabis users and created a sense of loyalty among them; now, it seems that the new mantra is *cannabis cash rules everything around me; for differentiation, see CCREAM*

open column extractor- *n.* ostensibly, this is a glass, metal or plastic tube that has a removable screen or filter on one end and a small hole at the other, and is filled with cannabis plant parts in order to blast them; *see Queen Bee Extractor, blast*

oregano- *n.* supposedly, the herb that was passed off as cannabis to cannanewbies and losers in the 1970s and 1980s; according to some old-timers, *oregano* was laced with cheap, chemical drugs like LSD or amphetamines and was marketed as cannabis on the street

Organic- *adj.* an owned term for having the quality of a specific type of licensed gardening; unfortunately, since it is an owned term, cannabis may never earn this designation; it's sad and stupid that we cannot have them verify that my medicine is as clean as my food; so far, the closest to *Organic* cannabis is *Clean Green Certified*; *i.e. Organic is a word not typically in the dictionaries in many agricultural towns found in the California Central Valley, New Jersey, and the Midwest.*

O' Shaughnessy's- *n.* a medical cannabis periodical named after William Brooke O' Shaughnessy, the man responsible for first introducing the therapeutic use of cannabis to Western medicine

ounce- *n.* the unit of measurement equal to twenty-eight grams; typically, cannabis is sold by the gram, by increments of eighths of an *ounce*, or by the pound; an *ounce* of cannabis retails for anywhere between $50 and $560 (yes... that is correct... I have actually seen the $560 *ounce* price for a strain at a ridiculous and ghetto California dispensary); also, *ounce* is the unit of measurement used to determine the quantity of heart or character of a certain politician; *i.e. It truly seems that Chris Christie doesn't have an ounce of compassion in his entire being...maybe he should blaze an ounce to his head.*

outdoor- *n.* any cannabis that is cultivated outdoors as opposed to indoors or in a greenhouse; due to the ignorant misconception that indoor cannabis is universally superior to *outdoor*, indoor cannabis is almost always more expensive than *outdoor* (unless the *outdoor* is grown by an exceptional cannabis cultivator, and then it can be set side-by-side on the same shelf with indoor and fool almost all weed nerds); top quality *outdoor* cannabis from certain regions is so drastically superior to indoor and cannabis from other areas that these regions will soon become appellations; —*adj.* having the quality or characteristic of *outdoor* cannabis; *i.e. Outdoor cannabis grown in the redwood-forest-humus-rich soil of Santa Cruz County has such a unique and distinct character that many, myself included, consider it to be the best cannabis on earth.*

oven- *n.* the bowl of a vaporizer or portable vaporizer; the final peace of mind Sylvia Plath so desperately desired; *for differentiation, see bowl, whip*

OZ- *n.* an ounce; in this case, it is pronounced like the wizard; *see ounce*

oz- *abbrv. see ounce*

ozone generator- *n.* a type of odor control device occasionally employed in large commercial grow ops that scrubs the air by producing ozone

ozzy- *n. see ounce*

pack- *v.* to fill a bowl or oven with cannabis; —*packed adj.* the state of being full of cannabis flowers ready for combustion or vaporization; *i.e. The bowl is packed, the Netflix is here... let's chiiiiiillll, girrrl.*

paddle- *n. see dab tool*

pakalolo- *n.* the Hawaiian word for cannabis that is used colloquially throughout the world... Mahalo!; *i.e. Why don't you go pack a bowl, ho, of that pakalolo, yo.*

Pakistani- *n.* an indica cannabis landrace originating in the Hindu Kush mountain range of Pakistan; one notable characteristic of *Pakistani* cannabis is that many genotypes present with flat stems instead of the typical cylindrical stems of other landraces and hybrids; *Pakistani* is great and all, but most people I know simply prefer *Packabowli*

Panama Red- *n.* a sativa dominant legendary heirloom cannabis strain of the *red* variety; there was a time that every cannabis sold was called either *Panama Red* or *Maui Wowie* (even though most of it was actually *Mexican* or Mexican-grown *Columbian*)

papers- *n.pl. see rolling papers;* where the name of this book is gonna be seen for weeks at the top of the bestseller list

papery- *adj.* having the characteristic of being light, slightly crispy, and somewhat artificial feeling like that which is often the ultimate presentation of indoor cannabis flowers or water-cured buds

paranoia- *n.* BOO!; the often valid, though inaccurately attributed, side effect of cannabis use; in fact, because cannabis opens your mind to the bright, frightening and limitless real world, you begin to get nervous about the government-sanctioned murderers in city-issued uniforms who could potentially bust down your door with ease over a motherfucking plant... and that shit, my friends, is enough to make any sane person experience *paranoia; see black pepper*

144

paraphernalia- *n.* a legal or grandparents' term for any ancillary item used in the consumption of cannabis, like a bong, papers, or a dab tool

parts per million (PPM)- *n.* the quantity of dissolved solids or salts in a cannabis nutrient solution as expressed by the number of molecules dissolved in one million parts of solution

party bowl (party-bowl)- *n.* a large bowl in a pipe or for a bong that holds more than one gram of cannabis and is typically intended for use when consuming cannabis in a group; *i.e. My morning routine consists of three party bowls of meds, a cup of lemon ginseng green tea, and a kiss from my beautiful wife... but not in that order.*

party size- *adj.* having the characteristic of a joint that is approximately one hundred and fifty millimeters long

passing the torch- phr. a euphemism for passing a joint; what Michael Phelps was good at before rehab

pass to the left- phr. the cannabis joint smoking etiquette that refers to the commonly accepted practice of taking two hits of a joint, and then *passing it to the left*; *see puff, puff, pass*

Patent US6630507- *n. see 6630507*

patient provider- *n.* the term California dispensaries give to members of their collective who also donate or vend flowers or other cannabis products in-house; in many areas, all providers at a given dispensary are supposed to be *patient providers,* though in the loosely regulated or grey markets this is not always the case

patient registry- *n. see voluntary patient registry*

peace- *n.* the ultimate outcome of entire, global legalization of the cannabis plant; *see bullshit*

peacenik- *n.* a conjunction of *peace* and *beatnik* formerly used to describe a peace-loving, poetry-writing pothead; *i.e. One could possibly describe Lennon as a peacenik.*

peace pipe- *n.* colloquial for a cannabis pipe, especially one that is passed among a group of friends and future betrayers who are aching to stab you in the back, steal your genetics for their own profit, and lie so profusely about you in the social media that everyone believes their bullshit instead of the truth

peat- *n.* peat moss; the main material used in soilless mediums designed for cannabis cultivation; *peat* should be avoided due to its environmental impact and its risk of causing damping off; *peat* can easily be replaced by coir; *see coir*

peat pellets- *n.pl.* small, compressed circles of peat wrapped in netting that are reconstituted with water to be used for germinating seeds or rooting cuttings; *for differentiation, see coir pellets, peat*

peer pressure- *n.* the negative and detrimental external force of influence from one's friends and family that aggressively encourages the use of lethal substances like pharmaceutical drugs and alcohol; the positive suggestion from a loved one that cannabis might be a safer alternative to the use of opiates and barbiturates and depressants and antidepressants and tobacco and caffeine and booze and sugar and...

percolator- *n.* a specific type of bong where the smoke is drawn through multiple chambers of water or ice; a good equatorial sativa wake and bake through a *percolator* is better than the best coffee ever

perlite- *n.* a form of buoyant amorphous volcanic glass formed by the heating and cooling of obsidian that is often used in cannabis potting mixes or as a stand alone hydroponic medium

Peron, Dennis- *n.* a cannabis legend and activist who, among many other notable accomplishments too numerous to mention herein, is partially responsible for authoring California's (in)famous Prop 215; thank you, Mr. Peron

per se **DUI laws-** *n.pl.* the group of states' laws dictating that the existence of cannabis in a person's system denotes legal intoxication without exception or any further assessment of impairment; *per se DUI laws* cannot work for cannabis given the rate of metabolism of the active cannabinoids by the human body; the presence of cannabis in the system is evidence of consumption, but not of intoxication, since it takes approximately thirty days to eliminate THC from the body; obviously, the effects of cannabis do not last days, but rather minutes or hours, and *per se DUI laws* are actually simple tools of torture employed by the War on Drugs machine

personal use- *n.* the use of cannabis by adults age twenty-one and over for any reason other than sale including but not limited to personal, recreational, meditative, spiritual, conjugal, religious, athletic, homeopathic, dietary, or other purposes within reason of the law; or, the possession of said cannabis on one's person or personal property

pesticides- *n.pl.* a group of products, most often composed of dangerous synthetic chemicals, used to repel, kill or prevent the infestation of insects, fungi or diseases; fungicides and miticides are types of *pesticides;* extremely toxic and poisonous *pesticides* are responsible for the recall of hundreds of thousands of cannabis products in Colorado, and are the primary evidence in the argument for regulations; certain *pesticides,* like organic cinnamon oil, organic lavender oil, and OMRI neem oil, are safe for use on cannabis; unfortunately, many cultivators are sociopaths who care more about their bottom line than they do about the health and safety of their clients; these cultivators use unsafe, often illegal, systemic *pesticides* and fungicides containing the neurotoxin imidacloprid or myclobutanil found in brands like Eagle 20 and Mallet; *see purge, dab, weed people*

pet the green gerbil- *phr.* what the fuck is this?; who would ever call smoking cannabis *petting the green gerbil*, especially since it sounds like stroking something rotten that crawled out of a skank's asshole

PGRs- *abbrv. see plant growth regulators*; not for use on cannabis; ever; ever, ever; never, never, never, ever!

pH- *abbrv.* literally, *potential hydrogen; pH* is used to designate the acidity or basicity of a cannabis nutrient solution or medium on a scale of zero to fourteen, with zero being the most acidic, fourteen being most basic and water being seven; cannabis should be cultivated in a medium with a *pH* range of 5.8-6.8, and be fed nutrient solutions that are no lower than 5.0 and no greater than 6.5 (with 5.5 being roughly ideal, depending on circumstances); in proper organic cannabis cultivation, water is still the best *pHed* solution

pharmaceutical- *n.* a prescription or over-the-counter medical substance synthesized in a lab in order to demonstrate that humans can create inferior knockoffs and copies of readily available medicines found in nature; virtually every single *pharmaceutical* available to the public is more dangerous or potentially lethal than cannabis and the vast majority of time-tested herbal remedies; *i.e. It only takes ten grams of the pharmaceutical acetaminophen to cause liver failure and death in the average adult human... just so the math is clear, that's twenty extra strength pain relieving pills available over the counter right now to anyone, or waiting in the cabinet for your toddler to stumble upon and mistake for breath mints. And you all keep fucking lying, saying pharmaceuticals are safer than cannabis.*

phatty (fatty)- *n.* an extremely large joint or blunt; typically, a joint cannot be called a *phatty* unless it contains at least an eighth of cannabis

phenotype- *n.* when it comes to cannabis, think about it like this: the genotype is the strain itself and the *phenotype* is a specific plant of that strain; the more genetically stable a genotype is, the fewer *phenotypes* present in the offspring

philly- *n.* a colloquialism for a blunt based on the cigar brand commonly purchased for the wrappers used to roll blunts

Phoenix Tears- *n. see Rick Simpson Oil, full extract cannabis oil*

phosphorous- *n.* along with nitrogen and potassium, one of the three major elements used by cannabis plants for growth and development; *phosphorous* specifically aids in the production of roots and initiates or increases flower development; although it is necessary through the entire life cycle, especially early for root development, *phosphorus* is the most readily available of the three elements and should be applied sparingly and only when there are signs of deficiency; *i.e. I rarely or ever have to apply extra phosphorus to my mediums.*

photoperiod- *n.* the amount of visible light or the visible light cycle available to a cannabis plant

phototropism- *n.* the act of a cannabis plant appearing to move towards the light as the sun travels across the sky over the course of the day

phytocannabinoids- *n.pl. see cannabinoid*

phytochemicals- *n.pl.* chemical compounds found in plants that are responsible for specific traits or functions (like color, smell, and pest resistance); these chemicals are typically helpful to humans, with some biological significance for healthy body function or disease prevention, resistance or cure; *phytochemicals* are not technically considered *vitamins*, but are documented to be hugely beneficial; one of the scientific justifications for natural and homeopathic medicines like cannabis

pick and mix (pick 'n' mix)- *n.* bulk cannabis seeds loosely labeled correctly that one can purchase online in quantities as low as one; *i.e. Due to the nature of cannabis genetics and their size, purchasing pick and mix seeds is a real crap shoot... quite often they are not the strain you ordered, but rather some random seed that probably fell on the floor of the packaging room in one of the large seed banks.*

piece- *n.* a device or implement used for smoking or vaping cannabis or cannabis extracts; *i.e. My favorite piece was a one-hitter carved from real ivory that I bought for twenty bucks at a swap meet in Watts.*

pied- *adj.* like the muthafuckin' piper; high or stoned; *i.e. Peter brought over a few pipefuls of Pineapple Cindy and we got pied as fuck.*

pinch- *n.* a very small amount of cannabis; also, the state of being without cannabis; *i.e. I've been in such a pinch before that I would have given my right nut for a pinch.*

pinch hitter- *n. see one-hitter*

pinchy- *n.* a small, usually glass, cylindrical straight pipe one-hitter

Pineapple Express- *n.* a mediocre cannabis movie staring Seth Rogen and James Franco that is centered around a mythical strain named, you guessed it, *Pineapple Express;* since the film's release in 2008, opportunistic breeding companies have sought to capitalize on the name's fame by releasing eponymous strains

pinene-*n.* a common terpene found in cannabis that has an astringent floral pine aroma; as it is one of the primary medical constituents of coniferous trees and rosemary, *alpha pinene* has undergone numerous scientific studies that have determined its efficacy as an anti-inflammatory bronchodilator and broad-spectrum antibiotic that can aid in memory; *pinene* is further proof that cannabis is indeed an invaluable medicine

pinner- *n.* a small joint; a joint so small that it must be held to the lips using a pin; this is not to be confused with a spinner… she is one who sits and spins on your other pinner; *i.e. I gotta smirk when I see cannabis clowns getting lit the fuck up from a pinner that wouldn't even make my grandma's head change.*

pipe- *n.* a device used for smoking cannabis that comes in many shapes, sizes and colors, just like the cocks many of them resemble; the defining characteristic of a *pipe* is that it is a tube with a mouthpiece or orifice at one end and a bowl for housing the cannabis to be combusted at the other

pipeful- *n.* the loosely quantifiable amount of cannabis that can be or is packed into the bowl of a pipe; *i.e. Packed with pipefuls of Gangsta's Paradise, me an' my girl bounced to some bumpin' DJ Snake beats.*

pistils- *n.pl.* the hairy part of the female flower that is designed to catch the male pollen; what are called *pistils* in cannabis aren't technically true botanical pistils, only the style and stigma; the so-called *pistils* are what give cannabis flowers that characteristic hairy appearance; also called *the hairs* on cannabis buds; a common misconception is that a bunch of orange hairs on a bud means that it is high quality

plant growth regulators (PGRs)- *n.pl.* synthetic and systemic poisonous chemical compounds designed to stunt the growth of ornamental trees and shrubs near utility lines; not safe for use on cannabis or food crops, and should never be used for those applications

plant limits- *n.pl. see possession limits*

plasma- *n. see light emitting plasma*

plug- *n.* any of a variety of small portions of starter medium, either rockwool, coir, or other organic conglomerate material that are used to germinate cannabis seeds or root cuttings; *plug* is not to be confused with Trump's rug, in which no cannabis could grow

pollen- *n.* the male reproductive grain equivalent to cannabis sperm; also, idiotically, *pollen* is also used as slang for kief; *i.e. Despite common perception among cannabis clowns, a pollen extractor should not be the name for a kief tumbler.*

pollen slingers (pollen chuckers)- *n.pl.* derogatory for amateur breeders, poor quality breeders, or breeders who find any and every male they can, pollinate every female strain they can buy, and then release the strains as stabilized genetics; quite honestly, nearly every expert breeder began as a *pollen slinger; i.e. He just said that the mullet man is a pollen slinger! Hahaha... that's so funny!*

polyhybrid- *n.* a cross or hybrid of more than two recognizable cannabis strains

popcorn buds (popcorn nugs, smalls)- *n.pl.* the small, usually older, cannabis buds at the bottom of a batch of flowers sold from a dispensary so named for their similarity in size and shape to popcorn; traditionally, *popcorn buds* are any small or medium-sized nug that still retains some semblance of quality despite its size; *for differentiation, see bottom buds; i.e. Honestly, I prefer popcorn buds to giant nugs of pretty trash, because the smalls have far less stem waste.*

poser- *n.* one who pretends or poses like they are a cannabis person, but is in fact only a dilettante; *i.e. The pro-recreational poser told me that I use too much medical cannabis, that no one could ever need that much, since cannabis really isn't medicine. Obviously, like most weed nerds, she has no idea what the fuck she's talking about.*

possession limits- *n.pl.* the arbitrary, often absurdly illogical, limits applied by legislation to the quantity of cannabis or cannabis products that a private citizen may possess or cultivate in a legal state; most often, *possession limits* are established by cannabis reformers or seasoned politicians who know too little about cannabis to ever possibly designate what is enough cannabis for another person; *i.e. It is fucking stupid logic to have possession limits set at six plants and one ounce of dried cannabis flower... like it is even possible to grow that little cannabis with six plants... what is one supposed to do with the other pounds of flowers off of the six plants? It seems like possession limits like these are actually encouraging the black market selling of cannabis.; see reformer, legalization, decriminalization, Adult Use of Marijuana Act*

post up- *v.* to get high and kick it in one spot for an extended period of time, often with a gangsta lean

pot- *n.* possibly the most common colloquialism for cannabis; *pot* is derived from an ancient cannabis-infused brandy drink called *potaguaya* or *potiguaya* (short for *poción de guaya*); what this country will continue to go to until we legalize cannabis nationwide; the container in which cannabis is cultivated is not called a *pot*, it's called a container; *for differentiation, see container*

potash- *n.* water-soluble potassium that is readily available for plant absorption; coincidentally, pot ash (cannabis ash) is high in potash

potassium- *n.* along with phosphorous and nitrogen, one of the three major elements used by cannabis plants for growth and development; *potassium* specifically aids in the production of flowers and increases cellular strength, flower size, and density; although it is necessary through the entire life cycle, *potassium* should be increased drastically during the flowering period of the cannabis life cycle

pot brownie- *n. see magic brownie*

pot cookie- *n.* a cannabis-infused edible cookie; this is not to be confused with *pot nookie*, which is sex after the consumption of cannabis

potency- *n.* the relative strength of cannabis or a cannabis product; the overall total level of cannabinoids in a cannabis product; often, *potency* is perceived to only be determined by the level of THC in a cannabis product; *i.e. The potency of my high CBD and high THC combination hybrids is out of this world.*

pothead (pot head)- *n.* one who consumes a great quantity of cannabis; a slightly lighter and more heady version of a stoner; *see stoner*

potluck- *n.* a gathering or party where guests bring an entrée and some cannabis for all attendees to enjoy; *i.e. The first time I went to a potluck was right after tripping balls offa mushrooms while listening to my homegirl play Moonlight Sonata on the ivory like a fuckin' boss.*

pot prophet- *n. see author*

pot shops- *n.pl.* the derogatory term for dispensaries or other cannabis businesses

pot shots (potshots)- *n.pl.* photographs of cannabis flowers, concentrates, or products; also, what weed people take at each other on the social media sites and forums

potting mix- *n.* a ready-to-use mix of amended potting soil and perlite that can be directly planted for most cannabis cultivation applications; *for differentiation, see potting soil*

potting soil- *n.* a ready-to-amend soil designed to be used as a base for potting mixes or as a soil conditioner to break up topsoil; *for differentiation, see potting mix*

pound- *n.* a unit of measurement equal to sixteen ounces of cannabis; usually, cannabis is sold by the gram, by increments of eighths of an ounce, or by the *pound*; a *pound* of cannabis retails for anywhere between $1,300 and $5,000; *see two thousand dollars*

PPM- *abbrv. see parts per million*

PPP (ppp)- *abbrv. see puff, puff, pass*

pre '98- *n. see Bubba Kush*

preflowers- *n.pl.* the small, individual flowers of discernable sex that appear at the nodes of sexually mature cannabis that is in its vegetative state; *preflowers* are used as an identification tool to determine the gender of a cannabis plant prior to the flowering period

preroll (pre-roll, pre-rolled joint)- *n.* a previously rolled joint, usually made with the house blend, that contains about one-half gram to one gram of cannabis and retails for ten to fifteen dollars at most dispensaries; occasionally, a dispensary will offer strain-specific *prerolls* at inflated prices, but this is often only their way to hide poor quality or otherwise compromised cannabis from an unsuspecting customer

press- *n. see oil press, hash press*

pretty trash- *n.* any cannabis or cannabis product that has an amazing appearance or looks good from a distance but is weak in potency, aroma or flavor; *i.e. The douchy dispensary owner stopped having his pretty trash tested, because it was always only eleven to fourteen percent THC.*

Project CBD- *n.* an organization founded by Martin A. Lee to promote the awareness of CBD as medicine and to provide an extensive source for finding medical documentation on the efficacy of cannabis; *see Lee, Martin A.*

propagate- *v.* to perpetuate a cannabis strain or cultivar through sexual or asexual reproduction

Proposition 215- *n.* the groundbreaking California legislation passed in 1996 that first legalized medical cannabis anywhere in the US; *for differentiation, see SB 420*

provider- *n.* any person or company who makes medical cannabis or medical cannabis products available to a verified medical patient or legal dispensary; *for differentiation, see dealer, patient provider, vendor*

psilocybin- *n.* the active component in hallucinogenic mushrooms; *psilocybin* can be medically viable like cannabis

psychoactive- *adj.* affecting the mind, mood or behavior; *i.e. Cannabis is considered to produce a psychoactive effect.; for disambiguation, see psychotropic*

psychoactivity- *n.* the quality or expression of quantifying how psychoactive a cannabis product is

psychopharmaceutical- *n.* a pharmaceutical drug that has a psychoactive effect on the user, often one prescribed to attempt to correct the ills of society through the swallowing of sickening synthetics; studies have shown that cannabis has a far greater (and safer) efficacy than most psychopharmaceuticals available to the paying public

psychotropic- *adj.* affecting the mind, mood or behavior; *psychotropic* and *psychoactive* are often used as direct synonyms, however *psychotropic* is the characteristic of a drug or other agent to cause a *psychoactive* effect on the brain

puck- *n. see hash puck;* this is not to be confused with your spritely friend who enjoys meddling with mischief in the cannabis love affairs of others

Puff- *n.* the Magic Dragon

puff- *v.* to breathe in cannabis smoke; to quickly and repeatedly draw cannabis smoke through a joint or pipe in order to feel the

156

effects more quickly or to initiate combustion; *for differentiation, see drag, draw*

puffer- *n.* one who smokes or puffs cannabis; also, a *puffer* can refer to a small pipe or one-hitter; this is not to be confused with a *fluffer* which is one who gets a *puffer* hard

puff, puff, pass (ppp, PPP)- *phr.* the description of the cannabis joint smoking etiquette dictating that one take two hits from a joint, *puff, puff,* and then *pass* it to the left (though, I've been told that it passes to the right south of the equator)

pumice (pumice stone)- *n.* extrusive volcanic rock that is used as an amendment in cannabis cultivation for its lightweight, neutral, and non-compacting aeration qualities; notably, *pumice* doesn't float to the surface of the soil or medium as readily as perlite; *see perlite*

purge- *v.* to (attempt to) remove the poisons, residual solvents, and toxins from cannabis concentrates; a physical impossibility; here's where all the concentrate makers are ignorant: no matter how much a concentrate is *purged*, remnants of the solvents remain, even in batches testing clean at a lab… see, the lab sets a minimum level that it deems safe, and there is no legal, scientific basis for these arbitrary designations… furthermore, even if the test comes back all zeros for residuals, that is simply a document saying that the specific sample the lab received is clean of only the substances for which the lab tests… what it doesn't show are the levels of any of a thousand other components that could be, and most likely are, present in the sample… what makes it worse is that fuel companies often have proprietary blends in order to differentiate their product from a competitor's, and there seem to be few laws dictating that they must list these (proprietary) ingredients on the MSDS… these blends are often unfit for human consumption, having side effects similar to that of inhaling industrial chemical fumes (huffing), and remain through most forms of *purging; i.e. According to a recent study, over 80% of concentrate samples in the test group were* *contaminated… so, it doesn't seem like they are doing a great job purging, does it?*

purging oven- *n.* a small, usually table-top, industrial, low temperature oven and vacuum combination that is designed to purge cannabis concentrates of residual solvents; *i.e. You know something is toxic if they have to sell specialty items like purging ovens in order to try to help themselves feel better about the probable dangers of the final product.*

Purple Erkel (Purple Urkle, Purple Erkle)- *n. see Granddaddy Purple*

Purple Haze- *n.* a legendary purple-hued sativa from the *Haze* line that was immortalized in the eponymous 1967 Jimmy Hendrix song

pusher- *n.* Propogandi *sadisti,* the extinct monster of the Scaremongering family that supposedly was known to force small children into extreme and severe addiction by pressuring them into using the psychosis causing devilweed called marihuana; the *pusher* demon was known to live by the mantra: *the first hit is free… after that, you're hooked*

pyrethrum- *n.* the insecticidal chemical derivative of the pyrethrum daisy, Tanacetum *coccineum,* that is used on cannabis to prevent or kill sucking, boring or mining insects

QP- *abbrv.* a quarter pound of cannabis flowers; often, a *QP* is the absolute smallest quantity of cannabis a dispensary would be willing to accept from a vendor or provider

quarter- *n.* a quarter ounce of cannabis; what we will not acquiesce in mercy unless the relentless prohibitionists surrender quickly and quietly

Queen Bee Extractor- *n.* a specific type of plastic butane honey oil extractor that is conical in shape and looks much like a rather large butt-plug (but is not recommended to be used as such)

QWISO- *acronym* quick wash isopropyl hash; *see ISO hash*

Rainy Day Women #12 & 35- *n.* the famous Bob Dylan song from 1966 that chants the mantra: *everybody must get stoned;* interestingly, the product of twelve and thirty-five is four hundred twenty

rasta- *abbrv.* one who is Rastafarian; —*adj.* having the characteristics of a Rastafarian or of a wannabe *rasta* who smoke di sacred herb; *see Rastafarianism*

Rastafarian- *n.* one who practices Rastafarianism; *see Rastafarianism*

Rastafarianism- *n.* a loosely defined religion or religious social movement like veganism that stems from the black Jamaican uprising against post-colonial oppression in the 1930s and was popularized in the cannabis community by Bob Marley

rasta hair- *n.* dreadlocks; a colloquialism for pube hairs that accidentally adhere to a cannabis flower; *i.e. Look out! Don't buy that shit... It's got rasta hair on it. That's so fucking gross!*

ratio- *n.* the proportion of one thing to another, usually represented by a colon; in terms of cannabis, *ratio* is used to describe the amount of THC to CBD a strain has, or the proportion of a certain nutrient to another in hydroponic cannabis cultivation; also, *ratio* can be used to describe the quantity of soil to amendments, or vice versa, in large-scale organic cannabis cultivation

raw- *n.* fresh cannabis; —*adj.* relating to fresh cannabis; also, *raw* can be used to mean high or stoned; *i.e. My girl got raw and then fucked me raw, because I grow great raw.*

reclaim- *v.* the dabber's equivalent of scraping a bowl or stem to smoke the resin

recommendation- *n. see verification*

recreational cannabis- *n.* any state-sanctioned cannabis intended for personal use with a desired effect or potential effect including but not limited to euphoria, orgasm, altered state of consciousness, relaxation, or loss of income

recycled glass stones- *n.pl.* an aerating amendment and medium occasionally used in cannabis cultivation as a more *environmentally friendly* alternative to other aerating amendments or stand alone media like rockwool; *for differentiation, see grow stones, rockwool, pumice, perlite*

redbud (red bud, red bricks)- *n. see Mexican brick bud*

red cannabis- *n.* a legendary line of cannabis sativas used by Dutch breeders in the 1970s and 1980s; cannabis strains having a red appearance or hue as opposed to a yellow, blue, green, silver or purple hue

red eyes- *n.pl. see bloodshot eyes*

red hair- *n. see hairs, pistils;* the color of follicular landscaping once adorning the terrain of my brain

reefer- *n.* old school for cannabis or one who uses cannabis; also, a joint rolled with cannabis flowers that often has kief, oil or hash added; *for differentiation, see oiler, tarantula*

reeferism- *n.* allusion, usually in text or speech, to cannabis by performing an intentional (though, possibly seemingly unintentional) slip-of-the-tongue usage of a cannabis term; *i.e. When I say 'Dank you very much' to the seventy-year-old cashier lady at the local five and dime, I am performing a reeferism. She digs it and always says back, 'You're welcome. Toke to you later...' which is fucking awesome.*

Reefer Madness- *n.* the 1936 film vilifying cannabis use and cannabis users as a warning to parents; modern day cult classic of the cannabis community viewed as a parody rather than as originally intended; —*reefer madness n.* the supposed insanity fallaciously attributed to cannabis use

reflux- *v.* in regards to cannabis, to *reflux* is to repeatedly wash cannabis plant material in slightly heated and repeatedly evaporated and condensed ethanol, isopropyl alcohol, or other similar solvent; in the creation of full extract cannabis oil, *refluxing* is often done for a long enough period of time to decarboxylate the cannabinoids simultaneous to the extraction process

reformer- *n.* the pretentious politically correct name for a cannabis activist who is financially solvent and completely or hereditarily connected within the cannabis industry; one who has a more intimate relationship with a microphone or a social media feed than they do with a shovel; one who wants change in the cannabis industry to make everything stay exactly the same and still earn them steadily increasing profits; one who doesn't know a Goddamn thing about cannabis, compassion, or the mechanics of people and politics; a member of a group that wastes countless hours and millions of dollars attempting to pacify everyone, including the prohibitionists; one who conspires to collaborate on the process of creating the roadmap for outlining the eventual bullet list of topics to potentially consider including in a future legalization measure or initiative possibly in 2016; a member of a group that took two years to do something poorly that my wife and I completed successfully, eloquently and ineffectively in ten days; one who cares more about the public perception of their narcissism or platform than they ever could care about cannabis or medical patients; the sincerest form of a cannabis poser; *see NORML, cannabis cup, activist, Blue Ribbon Commission, Adult Use of Marijuana Act*

regenerate (regen, rejuvenate)- *v.* to reinitiate the vegetative cycle of a cannabis plant directly following harvest of her flowers by immediately placing her stalk with some remaining vegetation under twenty-four hours of light

162

reggae- *n.* a genre of music originating in Jamaica in the 1960s that is said to be a direct descendent of *ska* and was popularized by Bob Marley; resultantly, *reggae* is often associated with cannabis use

Reggie (Reg, regs)- *n.* a colloquial term for regular, ordinary, or poorly grown cannabis flowers as opposed to top-shelf buds

regreen- *v.* to rotate the flowers in an already combusted bowl and turn any remaining unlit portion towards the top in order to ignite green material as opposed to slightly ashen shit

rejuvenate- *v. see regenerate*

rescue tabs- *n.pl. see tabs*

reservoir- *n.* the tub or basin used to store or hold a large amount of cannabis nutrient solution used in hydroponic applications; the enclosed portion of a bong, percolator, or rig that holds the water; also, *reservoir* can refer to a bud bimbo or goo goo doll's pussy

residual solvents- *n.pl.* any solvents or traces of solvent chemicals that remain in a cannabis concentrate after purging

resin- *n.* the oily secretion from the glandular trichomes on ripe cannabis; *resin* can refer to the oils that have been removed from a cannabis flower by heat and pressure, often called rosin; *resin* is also used to describe the residue in a bong or pipe that remains after smoking; in this usage, *resin* is the poor man's hash (I say *man* here because most women wouldn't be caught dead smoking that harsh-ass shit scraped outta the stem or bowl)

reversed- *adj.* having the characteristics of a cannabis flower that has been forced to change gender, usually from *female* to *male*, through some action or intentional external stressor; —*v.* to change the gender of a cannabis plant from female to male; *i.e. I reversed a cutting of my Lemon Crème (Lemon Jack x Sour Cream) strain with colloidal silver and used the reversed pollen* *on my grape candy phenotype of Purple Dragon Kush (Purple Widow x OG Kush) to create one of my all-time favorite hybrids, Prometheus.*

Rice, Ben- *n.* a notorious cannabis attorney in California who helped defeat the federal government in court for his client, WAMM; Rice helped make WAMM effectively the only federally *legal* medical cannabis provider in the nation; *see WAMM*

Rick Simpson Oil- *n. see full extract cannabis oil,* because that is all it is… he just used a recipe strikingly similar to one from the 1974 book by D. Gold, *Cannabis Alchemy,* named it *Rick Simpson Oil* or *Phoenix Tears,* and created a YouTube video demonstrating the process (which has earned him an immense amount of popularity and, presumably, trustworthy fiduciary financial gains)

ridin' dirty- *phr.* driving with cannabis, or other *contraband*; getting caught by law enforcement officers while driving with cannabis on one's person or in one's vehicle; *ridin' dirty* is not to be confused with what hippies do in old, beat-up Vdub bugs or buses

rig- *n. see dab rig*

rip- *n.* a hit or inhalation of cannabis smoke, usually from a bong; —*rip or rip it v.* to take a *rip* from a cannabis smoking device, usually from a bong; *see bong rip*

ripped- *adj.* high from taking (bong) rips

Rip-Shot Challenge- *n.* the hypothetical sociological experiment in human mortality and comprehension that pits a seasoned cannabis smoker against an admittedly seasoned alcoholic in a challenge of consumption; the rules are simple: for each bong rip the cannabis smoker takes (*Rip*), the opponent must take a measured one and a half ounce shot (*Shot*) of forty-percent alcohol like vodka or whiskey; the winner is the person who doesn't end up dead or in the hospital; I guarantee if any idiot were to participate in such a dangerous endeavor, the drinker will lose 100% of the time (and possibly lose his life more often than not); *i.e. Jason Porter Collinsworth would like to formally state that the Rip-Shot Challenge is fictional, and should not be attempted by anyone, ever. Collinsworth and his associates are not liable for the actions of anyone upon reading this satirical parody of a dictionary.*

RO- *abbrv.* reverse osmosis; a type of water treatment used in hydroponic cannabis cultivation where water flow is filtered and then divided into low or zero ppm water and waste runoff

roach- *n.* the butt or fag of a joint; the last few millimeters of a joint that is usually swallowed, discarded to the soil to feed future plants, packed in a bowl to be finished off, or consumed using the archaic tool of the troglodyte know as a *roach* clip

roach clip (roach-clip)- *n.* a small alligator clip, paper clip or other similar device used to prevent the burning of one's fingertips while consuming the roach of a joint; *i.e. Back in the day, only wusses used roach clips instead of their fingers... but they probably type better than I do nowadays.*

roasty toasty (roasted)- *adj.* stoned or baked

rocket- *n.* a cone or joint

rocket man- *n.* if one is to believe pop music, a *rocket man* is a homosexual cannabis smoker; *i.e. My old friend is a rocket man now married to another rocket man and they like to be called cock and socket men.*

rockwool (stonewool)- *n.* a hydroponic medium created from superheated rock that is spun into fibers like cotton candy; *rockwool* used to be the industry standard for hydroponic cultivation until the advent of coir

Rocky Mountain high- *n.* the state of being high or stoned on the US's first publicly available legal recreational cannabis in Colorado; the unfortunate precursor to an accidental resurgence in album sales of a narcolepsy-inducing songwriter with the eponymous hit folk song

Rodelization- *n.* the somewhat ridiculous name given to making feminized pollen by allowing nature to perform her natural cycles; simply put, it is *forcing* a female cannabis flower to produce a banana or a handful of bananas by letting it remain on the plant past the point of maturity or ripeness (which is what eventually occurs to virtually every female cannabis plant that isn't pollinated); *Rodelization* is considered by most cannabis authorities as the only natural way to produce feminized cannabis seeds, but is not a viable option for commercial seed production (no matter what some breeding companies claim, they can't possibly be doing this method to produce a commercial amount of seed for sale)

rogue hermie- *n. see ninja hermie*

rogue male- *n.* an errant male that slipped past examination and is now wrecking havoc on the ovules of your precious virgin cannabis flowers

roll- *v.* to twist cannabis together in a paper in order to create a joint

rolling papers- *n.pl.* the thin, usually glued, papers used to roll cannabis into a joint or cone; for cannabis consumption, only hemp *rolling papers* with a natural glue are recommended

rookie cookie- *n.* a cannabis cookie or other edible that is either lower in strength, or cut into a smaller portion, designed for consumption by a novice or cannanewbie; the term has since been adopted as a product name for a low-dose cookie by a company in Colorado; *rookie cookie* is not to be confused with *rookie nookie* which is sex between two virgins

166

rooting hormone- *n.* a synthetic plant hormone, usually indole-3 butyric acid or naphthalene-acetic acid, used to force a plant cutting to root; often, commercial *rooting hormones* are not safe for use on cannabis, and should be replaced with organic methods such as willow bark, honey, or azos

rooting powder- *n.* a powdered version of a rooting hormone compound; *for differentiation, see clone gel*

Rosenthal, Ed- *n.* a cannabis cultivation legend known for his numerous reference manuals and his *High Times* column, *Ask Ed*

rosin- *n.* the purest form of solvent-less, full-melt cannabis concentrate as it requires no solvent whatsoever, including water; *rosin* is made by applying high pressure and low heat to dried and cured mature cannabis flowers to force extract or extrude fresh cannabis resin; the downside of *rosin* is a moderate loss of terpenes to heat induced evaporation in the final product

rosin tech (rosin technique)- *v.* the official term created by the *inventors* that is used for the making of rosin; *i.e. What kids call rosin tech these days is what we called using a low-heat iron and parchment paper to press out the resin from buds in order to make great hash.*

RSO- *abbrv. see Rick Simpson oil*

RTU- *abbrv.* ready to use; in cannabis cultivation, *RTU* is commonly seen on the labels of pesticides and nutrients

ruderalis- *n.* a species (or subspecies) of cannabis that originates from the arctic areas, and the far north; because of the seasons with twenty-four hours of sunlight in these regions, *ruderalis* supposedly evolved from *indica* to flower automatically under any photoperiod less than eighteen hours

run (running)- *v. see blast*

S1- *abbrv.* the new botanical nomenclature used to signify the F1 of a selfed project, literally standing for *self one;* an *S1* is the offspring of a female cannabis plant that has been pollinated with feminized pollen from a cutting of the same plant; *i.e. An S1 is the equivalent of a human hermaphrodite fucking hermself to conceive a baby that is exactly like her famother.*

salad- *n.* colloquial for cannabis flowers; *i.e. Yo man, it's 420...wanna ditch this snitch and go get some salad?*

salt buildup- *n.* the result of applying too much synthetic, petroleum-based fertilizers or nutrients to a cannabis growing medium

salt-leeching solution- *n. see finishing solution*

S.A.M.- *acronym* for the devil; Smart Approaches to Marijuana; the oxymoronic name for a concerted group of likely honorable liars and immaculate, vicarious murderers led by evangelist Kevin Sabet; *S.A.M.'s* primary goal appears to be to ensure that the maximum number of people are hurt or have their lives otherwise damaged or ruined with the violence precipitated by The War on Drugs; presumably, the group gets its acronym due to the similarity between the logic of their propaganda and the intelligence of Sean Penn's character in *I Am Sam* when the two are juxtaposed

sample- *n. see lab sample*

samson (Samson, Sampson)- *n.* a colloquialism for a cannabis dealer; *i.e. Yo, Gregory, call samson up and get us some weeeeed, muthafucka. 'Sure thang, Delilah.'*

sand (beach sand)- *n.* high quality kief (or occasionally grated bubble hash) that gets its name from its characteristic look and color; high quality sand is usually 73 micron or less, but is most often 38 micron

Sanders, Bernie- *n.* the 2016 US presidential candidate most likely to legalize cannabis in the United States

sandwich- *n.* the euphemism used as a reeferism to cannabis by the characters in the hit television series that ended with a terrible, hateful, loathsome final episode; *see eating a sandwich*

Santa Cruz County, CA- *n.* the cannabis capital of the US based on four crucial pieces of evidence: *Haze*, Proposition 215, WAMM, and *Blue Dream*; *i.e. Denver, Humboldt, Oakland, Seattle, Miami, and Portland can suck it... Santa Cruz is the cannabis capital of the US.*

sap- *n.* a solvent-extracted cannabis concentrate somewhere along the continuum between shatter and nectar; *for differentiation, see cannabis sap, shatter, nectar*

sativa- *n.* a species (or subspecies) of cannabis that originates from tropical and equatorial regions; *sativas* have a stick or vinelike plant structure; hemp and high CBD strains are usually *sativa*; a common misconception is that *indicas* are higher in CBD than *sativas*, but most of the commercially available high CBD strains are *sativa* dominant; *sativas* tend to be more euphoric and giddy than indicas due to the presence of THCv, elevated levels of THC, and the presence of the more uplifting and invigorating terpenes like limonene

SB 420- *n.* the California legislation that clarified and expanded the rights and limitations of Prop 215; I include this entry simply to illustrate the walk that goes along with the talk: California is so cannabis-friendly as a whole that the legislators made the cannabis law number 420

scavenger smoker- *n.* a parasite of the lesser known Moochian family of Cro-Magnon humans who is characterized by his innate and insatiable ability to freeload cannabis from the greater Homo *sativan*

schnerfneefknoof (schnerf)- *n.* any unintelligible language used by one who is overly giddy from the effects of consuming a large quantity of cannabis or cannabis concentrate; *i.e. She was so baked that all she could do was laugh and blurt out a bunch of schnerfneefknoof.*

Schoenmaker, Neville- *n.* a legendary cannabis breeder from Australia who is responsible for opening the world's first cannabis seed company in the Netherlands, The Seed Bank of Holland; *Schoenmaker* is known as the father of Dutch seed banks and is responsible for the illustrious and world-renowned strain, *Neville's Haze* which is supposedly the seed version of the *Original Haze* from Santa Cruz, CA; *see Haze*

schwag- *n.* any fucking horrible cannabis; poorly grown cannabis; back in the day, *schwag* specifically referred to brick bud as opposed to greenbud

SC Labs- *n.* quite possibly the nation's most well-known and popular cannabis testing facility; *SC Labs* is continuously the lab used by *High Times* and other famous cannabis cups, but that doesn't necessarily make them the best

scoop- *n.* a shovel-shaped dab tool

scorched- *adj.* having the quality or characteristic of a cannabis plant or plant part that was burned or otherwise turned crispy from some sort of input or external stressor; a cannabis plant can appear *scorched* from light burn, excess nutrients, or from a lack of water; also, *scorched* is yet another colloquialism for being high, drunk, or both

score- *v.* to procure cannabis or cannabis products, usually in an illegal manner; *i.e. I had t' score from my creepy-ass neighbor cuz my usual gal, Shiyawntweeka, was outta town.*

scrape- *v.* to dig out or remove the resin from an implement, typically for the specific purpose of smoking the remains as a means to get a quick fix when it's dry around town; *for differentiation, see reclaim*

screen- *n.* a thin sheet of silk, steel, gold, nylon or polyester used to sift or separate cannabis concentrates from cannabis plant material; —*archaic* the metal netting placed at the bottom of a bowl to prevent ground or broken up cannabis pieces of brick bud from escaping into the stem to clog or otherwise complicate smoking; glass *screens* of sorts are available for use with glass pipes and bongs; —*v.* to use a *screen* to separate cannabis from its extractives

screen of green (SCROG)- *n.* a specific type of cannabis cultivation employed to maximize harvest yields and minimize plant count; in a *screen of green*, cannabis plants are topped, trimmed, and trained through a screen, trellis or fence over multiple weeks; *for differentiation, see sea of green, sea of screen of green*

SCRoG (SCROG)- *abbrv. see screen of green*

sea of green (SOG)- *n.* a type of cannabis cultivation where a large number of smaller cannabis cuttings are packed closely together over the growing area

sea of screen of green (SeaSCRoG)- *n.* a type of cannabis cultivation, typically outdoor, that combines the concept of sea of green and screen of green and is often employed by growers who want to maximize yields of a large variety of strains; in a *sea of screen of green* set up, large, screened or trellised cannabis plants with hundreds of bud sites are grown fairly closely together at a roughly uniform height across a small to medium plot of land

season- *n.* the period of the year, as in a growing *season*; —*v.* to prepare a nail for use prior to dabbing

seaweed- *n. see kelp*

secret agent- *n.* a joint that has been made from packing cannabis into an emptied cigarette tube in order to be smoked in public without the appearance of smoking cannabis, just the unmistakable aroma; *for differentiation, see vega*

seed- *n.* the encapsulated wonder and mystery of potential that begets every cannabis plant

seed bank- *n.* a distribution center for breeding companies; *for differentiation, see breeding company*

seeded- *adj.* full of seeds, usually mature seeds as opposed to those one might find in seedy cannabis; *for differentiation, see seedy*

seedfinder.eu (en.seedfinder.eu)- *n.* possibly the most comprehensive and accurate database of cannabis genetics available online, though they do need to update more often

seed selecting- *n.* the act of choosing the best quality, most mature cannabis seeds for germination, sale or donation

seed sexing- *n.* the act of looking at a cannabis seed and divining from its shape and movement what gender the resulting germinated plant will be; ridiculous bullshit pseudoscience quite possibly responsible for more lost genetics than damping off; given that cannabis seeds retail for an average of ten dollars a piece, *seed sexing* is a moronic idea that only a fool would follow; *i.e. I've probably sprouted more seeds than the person who invented seed sexing has ever even seen, and I tell you what: for every single one of his examples of seed types that are "guaranteed" to be male, I have grown a female plant.*

seedy- *adj.* full of cannabis seeds, usually ones that are immature or embryonic; *for differentiation, see seeded*

selective breeding (selecting)- *n.* the act of choosing specific cannabis plants for a specific trait or characteristic like purpling, pink pistils, high THC or CBD content, or flowering time

172

self- *v.* to create cannabis offspring from one mother plant using her own feminized pollen; —*selfed adj.* having the quality of selfing or being the product of self-breeding

selfed seed- *n. see self, S1*

sensi (sinse)- *abbrv. see sensimillia*

sensimillia (sensimilla)- *n.* cannabis that is grown without being pollinated and therefore has no seed; derived from the Spanish *sin semilla*, meaning *without seed*

Sensi Seeds- *n.* one of the greatest, most awarded, celebrated and prominent breeding companies based out of The Netherlands; it bears noting that they not only have a storied and illustrious strain catalogue, but *Sensi Seeds* also has singularly one of the most informative websites about cannabis

sesh- *n.* a cannabis smoking session; *i.e. Shhhh... there's a sess sesh in session.*

sess- *n.* colloquial for sensimillia

sex- *v.* to determine the gender of a cannabis seedling or cutting by examining the preflowers prior to force flowering; —*n.* the gender of a cannabis plant

sexual maturity- *n.* the state at which a cannabis seedling has developed preflowers that are visible to the naked eye on multiple nodes and is ready to begin flowering whenever the sun (or indoor cultivator) is

shake- *n.* the loose pieces of cannabis that have broken off of the dried flowers and collected in the bottom of the storage container; most often, house blend *shake* is used to fill prerolls at shady cannabis dispensaries

shake hands with God- *phr.* an apt and appropriate euphemism for getting high or consuming cannabis

Shakur, Tupac- *n.* the talented and famous West Coast rapper who supposedly got smoked in a bowl after he got smoked in the street

shatter- *n.* a specific type of cannabis concentrate that gets its name from the fact that it looks like it could *shatter* like glass

she- *pron.* unless explicitly talking about a male cannabis plant, *she* is the appropriate and industry standard pronoun for a cannabis plant or strain

Sherlock- *n.* a type of cannabis pipe shaped like the one famously used by a detective in some British novels; no shit

shit- *n.* an oxymoronic colloquialism for cannabis; —*shitty adj.* being fucked up on *the shit; i.e. I got some great shit this weekend that was the shit and got me shitty.; for disambiguation, see the shit*

shiva- *n.* colloquial for cannabis based on the association between the god Shiva and his use of cannabis to rejuvenate him from extreme family conflict

Shivaratri (Maha Shivaratri)- *n.* the ancient Hindu festival that celebrates the god Shiva with Prasad, offerings of cannabis

shmammered- *adj. see stammered*

shotgun- *v.* to inhale another person's exhalation of smoke while kissing her; the fourth sexiest thing one can do with cannabis and a woman (or partner)

shoulder tap- *v.* to ask completely random strangers if they know where you can score some weed, or if they can hook a brutha up with some nugs

shovel- *n. see scoop*

sift (dry sift)- *v.* to sieve cannabis material with a screen to make kief; occasionally, *sifting* is done with the addition of dry ice in order to expedite the separation of the kief from the plant material; —*n. see kief*

silica- *n.* an important mineral for cannabis cultivation that plants use for turgidity; often, *silica* is sold as a liquid solution of potassium silicate; organic sources of *silica* are horsetail and diatomaceous earth

Silver Pearl- *n.* a sativa dominant heirloom cannabis strain bred by Sensi Seeds that is *Early Pearl x Skunk #1 x Northern Lights*; she truly looks silver, and I miss the strain; it would be nice to have a real cutting of the *Silver Pearl* running around Northern Cali in the mid 1990s, or if Sensi would rerelease her in honor of this tome

Sisley, Sue- *n.* the famed psychiatrist who is noted for being granted by the federal government the rights to clinically study cannabis in the US, which promptly precipitated her being fired by the University of Arizona; *i.e. Any cannabis-friendly collegiate or potential collegiate should think long and hard before attending the University of Arizona because they fired Dr. Sisley for that shit.*

skins- *n.pl.* colloquial for rolling papers

Skunk (Skunk #1)- *n.* a uniquely balanced heirloom cannabis strain bred by Sensi Seeds that is a polyhybrid of Central and South American landrace cultivars, *Afghani* and *Thai*; as with *Northern Lights* and *Haze*, *Skunk #1* changed the face of cannabis and cannabis breeding forever; it truly smells like a skunk that repeatedly got run the fuck over on a freeway; *Skunk* is responsible for the stereotypical odor that prohibitionists associate with cannabis; *Skunk* was popularized in the late 1970s through the 1980s; fallaciously, several news agencies, including FOX News, have recently reported that there is a dangerous "new" type of marihuana [sic] called *skunk* with THC levels in the 10-14% range that is causing psychosis and schizophrenia in millions of ethnic Americans... wow, if my buds tested as low as 10-14% THC, I'd be embarrassed; if high potency cannabis is so detrimental, then how is it that I am able to so adequately and eloquently write this sardonic reference manual while smoking bong load after bong load of 25% THC cannabis?

skunky- *adj.* having the characteristic odor of *Skunk* cannabis

slab- *n.* a large sheet, brick or chunk of cannabis concentrate, specifically solvent-extracted concentrate; *i.e. No matter what you decide about dabbing, never choose to dab a slab!*

slanger- *n.* one who slangs; one who deals drugs on the black market; a drug dealer; i.e. *A politician is a slanger of lies.*

slide- *n.* the hollow shaft in a bong or dab rig that the stem or nail sits in and slips out of during the process of consuming cannabis or cannabis concentrates

small- *adj.* having the quality of being high or stoned as popularized on Saturday Night Live; —*v.* to get high or consume cannabis; —*smalls n.pl.* see popcorn buds; i.e. *Hey, mamma, after y'all land in SF we need to bounce somewhere to get small ona some smalls and fuck, jah know?*

Smith, Kevin- *n.* a writer, director, actor and producer of Hollywood films, many of which are pro-cannabis; *Kevin Smith* is noted for publicly supporting cannabis and for appearing on the cover of *High Times*; *see Jay and Silent Bob (and see Dogma and Clerks and Chasing Amy and Mallrats... they are awesome)*

smokable- *adj.* having the characteristic of cannabis that can be smoked or vaped instead of consumed orally or applied topically; —*smokeable n.* a cannabis product that can be smoked

smoke- *v.* to combust cannabis and inhale the vapors; —*n.* a colloquial term for cannabis intended to be smoked *smoke an L-* phr. see L-plate

smoke expansion- *n.* the characteristic of the smoke of certain strains that is defined by a seemingly disproportionate increase in the volume in one's lungs after inhalation

smoke out- *v.* to smoke cannabis; most often in context, *smoke out* is combined with a plea and the pronoun *me*; *i.e. Hey man, I'm broke as fuck... can you smoke me and my girl out? 'Yeah, bro, I'll smoke you out this time.'*

smoke two joints- phr. see Sublime

smoking etiquette- *n.* the more or less universal set of guidelines for smoking cannabis with others; examples of cannabis *smoking etiquette* are: when smoking a joint in a group, take two hits with dry lips (no slobbering on the tip) and pass it to the left; whenever smoking cannabis in a group, always pass the piece or joint to the left; no matter how high you get, be mindful enough to keep passing instead of bogarting; when smoking with a group of four or fewer people, divide the green hit so that each person gets a portion of the green; when passed an empty bowl or one that is near the ash hit, repack it, take the first hit, and pass it to the left; if you empty the bowl or take the last hit, pack it again for the group unless you were previously the last one to do so; when going to a party where cannabis is expected to be consumed, bring cannabis flowers or the equivalent in products in order to be an equally contributing member of the group... money does not qualify: buy your shit before you get to the gathering; refrain from bringing your entire garage in a tool or tackle box in order to dab; if one must dab, bring a traveler or other easily passable device and a small kit; refrain from ninja dabbing anyone, ever; if you happen to accidentally break someone's piece, replace it with one of greater value within forty-eight hours or suck their dick in compensation; when smoking in a group, ensure that everyone gets a chance to hit the green and fulfills his obligation to pack a green bowl; when smoking from a bong, always clear the chamber prior to passing it on and never drool in the opening; bring your own lighter and don't jack anyone else's; if presented flowers from a grower, no matter the quality, do not say that your flowers are better, or that you know a great grower who is better than they are… simply take the flowers, say thank you, and find something to compliment them on or change the subject; *i.e. Many cannanewbies need to be taught smoking etiquette.*

smokin' grannies- *n.pl.* grandmothers who consume cannabis; also, hot grandmas who consume cannabis; *i.e. I just got blazed with some smokin' grannies in their early forties.*

smot poker- *n.* dyslexic for *pot smoker; smot poker* is not to be confused with a *smock poker,* which is someone who likes to make fun of pharmacists for selling so much poisonous shit that could be replaced with cannabis

snap- *n. see shatter*

snap it through- phr. to suck the ash of a bowl through the stem into the reservoir of a bong

Snoop (Snoop Dog, Snoop Lion)- *n.* cannabis hero and rap legend who has a difficult time deciding on a handle; one of the world's most recognizable and talented cannabis advocates

soarin' (soaring)- *adj.* flying high from cannabis consumption

soda popping- *v.* spraying or dipping blasted buds in soda or lemonade and then drying them to give the cannabis flowers the (false) appearance of still having the crystals that had been removed during the running process; *i.e. I caught the delivery owner blasting and soda popping his buds so I blasted his name on the grapevine.; see blast*

SOG- *abbrv. see sea of green*

soil aerator- *n.* a soil conditioner or amendment that provides room for oxygen in the medium

soil conditioner- *n. see amendment*

soilless medium- *n.* a medium used in cannabis cultivation that is free from the burdens of nature and the complicating confines of soil; typically, *soilless mediums* are made with peat, coir or redwood bark

solvent- *n.* a chemical liquid or liquid gas that removes active cannabinoids from cannabis; water is technically a solvent, but is rarely grouped in the category since many of the other solvents can be extremely toxic and can rarely be completely removed from the final concentrate

solvent-less (solvent-free)- *adj.* having the characteristic of being made without the use of any solvent other than water, as in *solvent-less* cannabis concentrates like rosin or bubble; the term was popularized by extract artist and prestigious pulpiteer, NikkaT

soul- *n. a joint rolled in toilet paper,* according to George Clinton anyway

Sour Diesel (Sour D, ECSD)- *n.* a sativa dominant cannabis strain that is an off-shoot of *OG Kush, Chem '91, Super Skunk, Northern Lights* and/or *Skunk VA*, depending on which hype one chooses to believe; what is known for sure is that *Sour Diesel* has an unmistakably pungent aroma of sour citrus and diesel fuel

souvenir seeds (souvenir cannabis genetics)- *n.pl.* cannabis seeds purchased from internet seed banks, called *souvenir seeds* so they can slip right through the legal loophole and be distributed; *see Attitude Seeds, Herbies*

sow- *v.* to plant cannabis seeds for the purpose of germination

Soxhlet extractor- *n.* a specific type of laboratory extractor usually made from glass that is used to distill full extract cannabis oil

soybean meal- *n.* an amendment occasionally used in cannabis cultivation that is composed of ground soybeans and contains a high percentage of nitrogen; if using *soybean meal* for cannabis cultivation, make sure that it is non-GMO

space cadet (space case)- *n.* a slightly derogatory term of endearment for a low IQ cannabis user, or one who is notoriously spacy or flighty after cannabis consumption

space cake- *n.* cannabis-infused cake

space cowboy- *n.* a cavalier space cadet

spank stank- *v.* to smoke cannabis hard, really fucking hard, so hard it leaves a mark

Spannabis- *n.* the world-renowned cannabis cup held annually in Barcelona, Spain

spark- *v.* to light or combust cannabis flowers or concentrates; *i.e. If you don't spark that joint up, I'm gonna spark this bowl right here and smoke it to my head.*

sparkita- *n.* an endearing or affectionate term for a female, especially one in her twenties, who likes to smoke a large quantity of cannabis

sparky- *n.* a pedantic or affectionate term for a male, especially one in his twenties, who likes to smoke cannabis

spectroscopy- *n.* the method of testing cannabis flowers and concentrates by using light to determine the potency

speed weed- *n.* cannabis that is highly stimulating rather than sedating, often due to elevated levels of THCv (or THC); *i.e. I adore a good speed weed in the morning before I write.*

spice- *n.* an extremely dangerous synthetic-cannabinoid-laced plant material intended as a legal (and therefore *safe,* of course) alternative to cannabis; responsible for more deaths this year alone than cannabis has in its entire history

spider mite- *n.* a sucking, web forming insect of the Tetranychidae family that colonizes the undersides of cannabis leaves; a *spider mite* infestation can be devastating to a cannabis garden, and must be monitored and controlled for well

spliff- *n.* a large joint or cone, usually rolled with three or more grams of high quality cannabis flowers, that is smoked to one's head (alone); the qualifier is the defining factor of what makes a *spliff* a *spliff* instead of just a big ass joint; *i.e. Pass me that spliff, yo! 'Nah, mon, if I did it'd no longer be a spliff so I's gots to keep this shit right here.'*

spliffted (upspliffted)- *adj.* high from a spliff

squinty-eyed- *adj.* having the characteristic of being so stoned that one's eyes are barely open even when fully awake

stab- *v.* to take a dab off a hot knife; *see hot knife*

stabilized- *adj.* having the characteristic or quality of cannabis genetics that are identical in offspring due to generations of selective breeding

stammered- *adj.* a conjunction between *stoned* and *hammered* that refers to being both drunk and stoned; *i.e. The party animal stammered more, because he was fucking stammered. Not sssmssmsmart.*

stash- *n.* one's personal collection of cannabis

Steep Hill Labs- *n.* a large cannabis testing lab chain with locations in California, Colorado, Nevada, New Mexico, and Washington

stem- *n.* the shaft in a bong or for a bong that the bowl sits on; a natural, lip-numbing toothpick; —*stemmy adj.* having the quality or characteristic of cannabis flowers that have too much stem; often, *stemmy* cannabis is either grown in a low-light situation or is not well-manicured, or both

sticks 'n' stones- *n.pl.* a colloquialism for Mexican brick bud based on the fact that there is a great percentage of seed and stem in said cannabis; *i.e. Sticks 'n' stones don' never get in my cones, and you homies can't ever outsmoke me!*

sticky- *adj.* having the characteristic of cannabis flowers that are tacky to the touch; properly cured cannabis is slightly *sticky*

sticky icky icky- *phr.* the description for cannabis flowers that are tacky and pungent that was popularized by Snoop

stoned- *adj.* having the quality or condition of being severely altered by cannabis such that it causes sedation and relaxation as opposed to the invigorating euphoria captured by the term *high; i.e. Blackberry Kush is one of those strains that always gets me stoned as fuck and puts me to sleep... I don't like that. I prefer to be able function, so give me my speedy sativas.*

stoned rabbits- *n.pl.* a group of feral rabbits who would get stoned off eating cannabis leaves if Utah were to pass legislation to legalize medical cannabis... at least according to genius DEA agent Matt Fairbanks, who obviously cares more about the mental state of a hare than he does about the wellbeing of terminally ill children; one of many debunked scare tactics used by ridiculous prohibitionists as a means to pull on the heart strings of unsuspecting PETA members who are also cannabis consumers; *i.e. It is sad that I know so much more than these officials who are supposed experts, and they just keep spitting bullshit at us like these stoned rabbits... from eating cannabis leaves...that haven't been decarboxylated... so, I guess, actually, they are magic rabbits with mystical decarboxylating stomachs that some ganjapreneur better capitalize on quickly!*

stoner- *n.* derogatory for a person who consumes, smokes or vapes a large quantity of cannabis, usually to the point of incapacitation, on a daily basis; it is important to note that the *stoner* stereotype holds true to a certain extent, but is not actually the direct result of excessive cannabis use; typically, a *stoner* is lazy, lacks motivation, and is gluttonous, but these are all traits of people brought to the surface by cannabis (if they weren't using cannabis, they'd still be lazy, unmotivated gluttons); also, a *stoner* by definition consumes a large amount of cannabis, but not all people who use cannabis heavily are *stoners*; *stoner* is not to be confused with a character in *The Lottery*

stonewool (stone wool)- *n. see rockwool*

stoney- *adj.* having the characteristic or quality of being nearly stoned, a little stoned, or high and stoned; *see stoned; i.e. The sun's goin' down an' I'm feelin' a little stoney an' it's gonna be a good night tonight, alright!*

stoney macaroni- *n.* a juvenile euphemism for cannabis-infused pasta; also, *stoney macaroni* is a bastardization of *stoney maroni; see stoney maroni*

Stoney Maroni (stoney maroni)- *n.* the universal pseudonym given to one who is high or stoned, or one who is frequently or continuously stoned or high; *i.e. In college, my nickname was Stoney Maroni;* when used as an adjective, *stoney maroni* simply refers to the state of being stoned or high; *i.e. Stoney Maroni was definitely stoney maroni this morning.*

straight pipe- *n.* a type of pipe that has no obstruction, water, or other filtration; according to recent studies, the *straight pipe* is purportedly the safest, healthiest mode of ingesting cannabis smoke

strain- *n.* a named type or variety of cannabis, usually from a specific breeder, but occasionally only available as a cutting, cultivar, or clone; for clarification and classification purposes, when a *strain* is cited in an academic, journalistic, or professional source, the name must be italicized; —*v*. what you have to do to see the trichomes on poor quality cannabis

strain hunter- *n*. one who searches and scours the globe looking for rare, unique or prized landraces and varieties of cannabis; great breeders are consummate *strain hunters*, always striving to find the best cannabis to use in projects (not just the trendy strains with the most popular name)

Strain Hunters- *n*. a documentary series released by Green House Seed Co. chronicling Arjan, Franco, and Simon's quest to find the world's greatest strains; the breeding company begot by the documentary

strain-specific- *adj*. having the quality or characteristic of an edible, preroll, topical or other cannabis product that is supposedly made with only one recognizable strain; dispensaries often offer *strain-specific* items in order to make more money on the hype of a fad; some places do this so they can claim to give patients the opportunity to choose products that are honestly-really-truly-for-sure-trust-them *strain-specific*

strap- *n*. *see molasses;* —*strapped adj*. having the characteristic of cannabis that has been fed molasses; also, the characteristic of one's wallet after purchasing top-shelf cannabis

stress- *n*. colloquial for schwag or brick bud, as it causes undue stress to remove all the seeds and stems; —*v*. to cause trauma to a cannabis plant through some sort of external influence like irregular light schedule, colloidal silver, or throwing her out of a motherfucking window; *i.e. Don't turn your beautiful buds to stress because you stressed them too much.*

stretch- *v*. to lengthen towards the light, typically when being forced to flower; when the light cycle of an indoor garden is changed to twelve-twelve, cannabis plants will usually *stretch* abruptly before beginning to pack on flowers

Stroup, Keith- *n.* cannabis legend and founder of NORML; famed for the mantra: *It's normal to smoke pot.*; *see NORML*

stuck- *n.* the condition of being unable to move or interact due to excessive cannabis consumption; often, *stuck* is the way a cannanewbie feels when she is *in a movie* or experiencing couchlock; *see in a movie, couchlock*

stuff- *n. see shit*

Sublime- *n.* a (now ghostly) band that once was popular before the death of their legitimate lead singer and is still famous for suggesting to everyone that they smoke two joints before doing anything and everything; *i.e. All my housemates cried and played Sublime for weeks when Bradley passed away.*

substrate- *n. see medium*

sugar leaf- *n.* bud leaf; leaves in and around the ripe cannabis flowers that are covered with glandular trichomes, giving the appearance of a sugar coating; mmm, candy-coated yumminess; *sugar leaf* is often used by manufacturers to make lower grade concentrates and medibles

Sunset Sherbet (Sunset Sherbert)- *n.* an indica dominant cannabis strain supposedly bred by the Cookie Family that is *Girl Scout Cookies x Pink Panties;* I only include this listing to illustrate the ridiculousness of the cannabis trends... how can the latest fad be the same dress as the previous year just with different underwear? What are all the contemporary breeders, fashionistas?

sunshine- *n.* a beautiful, reverent colloquialism for cannabis flowers, especially sativas or strains with bright terpenes like limonene

Sunshine #4 (Sunshine Soilless Mix #4)- *n.* singularly the most popular soilless hydroponic or indoor growing medium in the cannabis industry; although *Sunshine #4* is known for its quality, uniform ingredients, the medium seems to be behind the times: *Sunshine #4* is predominately composed of peat, which is not a sustainable or renewable resource like coir; also, peat can create a soggy, acidic medium… both of which cannabis despises; if one is going to resort to hydroponics, a more environmentally friendly and less expensive choice could be to make one's own medium from coir, perlite, pumice, vermiculite, microbiologicals and a trace amount of lime; *i.e. I'd like it if they were to come out with Sunshine #77, made with all organic, sustainable and neutral ingredients like coconut coir and without peat.*

super size- *adj.* having the characteristic of a joint that is approximately one hundred and seventy-five or more millimeters long; *super size* is not to be confused with having the quality of unhealthy obesity perpetuated by celebrating the plus-size hypertension heroes parading around in their sweaty cottage cheese and muffin tops spilling out of way-too-small thongs or bikinis trying to convince everyone that it is okay to be obscenely and appallingly overweight… the inverse of anorexia is equally as unhealthy, isn't it?

surfactant- *n.* a compound used to lower the surface tension between a liquid and a solid, specifically used as a wetting agent and dispersant in cannabis growing mediums, nutrients, fertilizers and foliar sprays; some common *surfactants* used in cannabis cultivation are yucca and Quillaja *saponaria*

sweet leaf- *n.* cannabis or cannabis trim; *see sugar leaf, trim*

Sweet Tooth- *n.* a balanced cannabis strain bred by Barney's Farm that is a polyhybrid of *Afghani, Nepalese and Hawaiian;* what some people get when they smoke cannabis

Swerve- *n.* the breeder handle of the head of The Cali Connection breeding company; although famous for various strains including *SFV OG*, he seems to have a knack for occasionally interchanging the mother and father when citing his breeding projects; *see genetics*

swing- *n.* a specific type of dab rig where the concentrate is placed on a metal or ceramic plate that is swung under an orifice for the vapor to be sucked through the chamber like one might expect in a Dr. Seuss book about douchy dabbing Doolittles who boo when visiting the true High Who (you know who) in Whohighville; also, the plate on which the dab is placed on a *swing*

synthetic- *adj.* unnatural; created in a laboratory instead of by God or Mother Nature; in terms of cannabis, virtually everything *synthetic* is poisonous; *i.e. Synthetic, petroleum-based fertilizers are poisonous to us, our soil, and our plants and should be avoided at all costs.*

synthetic cannabinoid- *n. see Marinol; for differentiation, see cannabinoid*

tabs- *n.pl.* cannabis-infused dissolvable tablets designed to quickly melt in the mouth as a means of rapidly administering cannabis medicine without the dangers of smoking or the side effects of tincture solvents like alcohol and glycerin; *for differentiation, see caps*

tackle box- *n.* the dabber's purse; the box in which many dabbers carry their rig, torch and concentrates; dabbers need a *tackle box* because of all the accoutrement required to perform the task of dabbing; *i.e. I like to walk by and laugh at the all the tackle boxes floating through the crowds at the cups. It would be plausible to think that one might mistake a cannabis cup for a bass fishing event. Plus, why does it take you all that shit to get high? All I need is cannabis and fire and I can get lit.*

taffy- *n.* a type of solvent-extracted concentrate so named due to its consistency… and the laughing it precipitates

Tahoe (Tahoe OG)- *n.* an indica dominant hybrid (or phenotype) of *OG Kush* from Tahoe, California, in the late 1980s; the *Tahoe* cut was used by Swerve in Cali Connection breeding projects; some people believe the *Tahoe* cut to be the mother of all *OGs; for differentiation, see OG Kush*

tamp (tamp out)- *v.* to use one's lighter, finger, or other device to squelch out or suffocate a cherry, or a smoldering or combusted bowl of cannabis; often *tamp* will be used in the common cannabis phrase: *tamp out the cherry; i.e. People always look at me crazy when I use a nickel to tamp out the bowl, but what the fuck… it's the right size.; see cherry*

tarantula- *n.* a large cone or joint that has been dipped in oil and rolled in hash and kief so named for the hairy, amber look it bears like that of a tarantula's leg; *tarantula* has since been adopted by a company as the name of one of their preroll products

TDS- *abbrv. total dissolved solids*; one of the ways the concentration of a cannabis nutrient solution is determined; *i.e.*

Since I grow biodynamic cannabis, I have never even used a TDS meter.

tea (T, big T)- *n.* a colloquial term for cannabis that is high in THC

teen- *n.* a sexually mature cannabis plant from seed or cutting; a *teen* clone is usually one that has a minimum of five nodes and is at least ten inches tall

temple balls (Nepalese temple balls, temple hash)- *n.pl.* large, hand-formed balls of hashish used in sacramental rituals in Nepal and other areas; *temple balls* are usually about the size of a large golf ball or baseball and can be spherical, ovoid, or cuboidal in shape

terpene profile- *n.* the collective group of terpenes for a specific strain; the unique aroma profile of an individual plant; what is used to determine a strain's fingerprint; *terpene profile* can make or break a strain; *i.e. If the terpene profile smells like shit, you won't want to smoke it no matter how great the cannabinoid profile is.; see cannabis fingerprint*

terpenes (terps, turps)- *n.pl.* aromatic organic compounds produced in the glandular trichomes; *terpenes* are the major medical components of cannabis resin aside from the cannabinoids; *terpenes* work synergistically with cannabinoids to produce a greater overall medicinal effect and are also responsible for cannabis' characteristic pungent aromas; many *terpenes* have documented medical benefits independent from cannabinoids (for example, beta pinene has antibacterial and other medical properties); *terpenes* are why flowers are the most potent and holistic form of cannabis medicine, and are further scientific evidence in the support for whole-plant legalization

terpenophenolic- *adj.* having the characteristic of a plant like cannabis that contains, produces or releases terpenes and phenols; *see terpenes*

terpineol- *n. adj.* a common terpene found in cannabis that has an floral lilac aroma; as it is one of the primary medical constituents of petitgrain, cajuput and pine, *terpineol* has undergone numerous scientific studies that have determined its efficacy as powerful sedative; *terpineol* is further proof that cannabis is indeed an invaluable medicine

terp juice- *n. see nectar*

testing- *v. see cannabis lab testing*

testing lab- *n. see cannabis lab*

tetrahydrocannabinol (THC)- *n.* the most commonly known psychoactive cannabinoid in cannabis that has antiproliferative, analgesic, antiemetic, appetite stimulant, and antispasmodic properties; there are three major forms: delta 8, delta 9, and delta 11, each with a unique action on the cannabinoid receptors in the human endocannabinoid system; *tetrahydrocannabinol* increases the efficacy of cannabidiol, cannabichromene, and cannabigerol; it is an antagonist of tetrahydrocannabivarin; THC: The High of Cannabis

tetrahydrocannabinolic acid (THCa)- *n.* the chemical precursor to tetrahydrocannabinol that must undergo decarboxylation in order to become THC

tetrahydrocannabivarin (THCv)- *n.* a psychoactive cannabinoid homologue of THC, and THC antagonist on CB1; one of the few cannabinoids that is not a derivative of CBG; found commonly in equatorial sativa strains, *THCv* has anorectic, bone stimulant, antiepileptic, and neurostimulant properties; *tetrahydrocannabivarin* is a natural weight-loss supplement that is safe and nontoxic for virtually all adults; did you hear that ladies? *i.e. When I started smoking high THCv strains, I lost over twenty pounds during a six-week summer vacation… and I kept it off.*

textile strain (fiber strain)- *n.* any strain, variety, cultivar or landrace of cannabis that is produced for its fiber content rather than for its cannabinoid content; interestingly, as cannabis has become more widely legalized, and hemp has again become one of the world's preeminent crops, agricultural scientists are finding that certain drug strains are actually better *textile strains* than the current best of the best available to hemp farmers; *for differentiation, see drug strain*

Thai- *n.* a sativa cannabis landrace from, you guessed it, Thailand

Thai Sticks- *n.pl.* a traditional form of prepared cannabis from Thailand that was popularized in the 1960s and 1970s; *Thai Sticks* are formed by leaving high quality, seedless cannabis flowers attached to their stems, and then securing them in place with remnants of fibers from the stem cuts; they were noted for their strength in comparison to the seeded cannabis that was readily available at the time; contemporary cannabis clowns cannot leave anything alone and have since given *Thai Sticks* the connotation of "buds on bamboo sticks dipped in hash oil"

That '70s Show- *n.* the famous sitcom that brought sitting in a circle in a smoky basement into the living rooms of millions of people

THC- *abbrv. see tetrahydrocannabinol*

THCa- *abbrv. see tetrahydrocannabinolic acid*

THCv- *abbrv. see tetrahydrocannabivarin*

The Emperor Wears No Clothes- *n. see Herer, Jack*

The Joker- *n.* a song by Steve Miller Band that made the word *toker* infamous; *i.e. My nickname used to be The Joker, because I cracked wise, smoked cigarettes, and toked a shitload.*

The Love- *n.* a sativa dominant cannabis strain cultivated by Love Genetics that is an *ACDC* phenotype with a high CBD ratio; the company donated several cuttings of *The Love* and of *ACDC* to WAMM, and now hundreds of sick people have access to a powerful medicine that they previously didn't have; in fact, there is a sign at the WAMM garden that reads "Love Grows Here," and this donation made sure they were telling the literal truth

the shit- *n.* irony; the best of the best of the best cannabis; *i.e. That Forbidden Love is the shit!*

The Unrevealed- *n.* the first cannabis superhero adventure novel of its kind; *The Unrevealed* follows the daily life of a hardcore cannabis breeder and apothecary who suddenly discovers that he has superpowers

thick smoke- *n. see creamy smoke*

thin film vacuum- *n.* the purging process or technique that is done by putting a thin layer of fresh cannabis extract in a purging oven; *see purge*

tide sticks- *n.pl.* cannabis colas that have been stored in a washing machine or a clothes dryer to prevent detection by the law or other authority figure; *i.e. Did your parents find your buds? 'Nah, I made that shit tide sticks and they found nuthin.'*

tight- *adj.* the antonym of airy; in terms of cannabis flowers, *tight* describes the proximity of flower clusters to each other: the closer or more densely packed it is, the more *tight* a flower will be after curing; *i.e. Everyone gets off over a tight flower.*

tincture- *n.* a liquid extraction of cannabis that is used sublingually and then swallowed for a combined medicinal effect; the medicine is absorbed and metabolized through the mucus membranes in the mouth to produce an effect similar to that of smoking; plus, swallowing the *tincture* causes the stomach and liver to metabolize the drug for additive effect; a *tincture* is made from alcohol; a glycerin solution is often labeled a *tincture* in most dispensaries and is for those who like their medicine untainted by ethanol

tissue culture- *n.* the practice of taking small samples of vegetative growth from a live cannabis plant and then suspending them in a sterile medium, like agar, in order to later be reincarnated through the application of specific plant hormones into a whole new Frankenstein...er...plant; although the practice is questionable in its use of synthetic plant hormones, it does provide the benefit of numerous disease-free offspring from very small tissue samples; *i.e. I like to call tissue culture cuttings Frankenplanten.*

titrate- *v.* to continuously, and often simultaneously, measure and adjust one's level of cannabis consumption based on the effects of the cannabis in order to balance or maintain dosage; unlike with alcohol or pharmaceuticals, cannabis, when smoked or vaped, is readily and easily *titrated* by the user or patient (though edibles are far more difficult to *titrate* and should at first be used with caution)

TMV- *abbrv. see tobacco mosaic virus*

to root- *v.* to force a cutting of a cannabis plant to grow roots in a moist medium through the application of a root-stimulating hormone or bacteria, or by the use of aeroponic stimulation on the cut portion of the stem

to the head (to my head)- *phr.* the act of smoking all of the cannabis by one's self; simply taking a large hit or consuming a great quantity of cannabis is technically not *to the head,* but is often used in that context; *i.e. Don't hate... I smoked an eighth L-plate to my head and I feel great.*

toasted (toasty)- *adj. see stoned*

tobacco mosaic virus (TMV)- *n.* an incurable and systemic plant disease that causes stunted or deformed growth, mutations, and chevron patterning on the leaves; the *tobacco mosaic virus* is spread through contact with cigarette or cigar smokers, with the use of nicotine pesticide sprays, or by insects that have been in contact with infected tissue; *TMV* does not leave a plant, nor its cuttings or seeds; the only way to eradicate or minimize the presentation of *TMV* is through selective breeding based on Darwinism, or supposedly through tissue culture; *i.e. The tobacco mosaic virus is the herpes of cannabis.*

toke- *v.* to smoke cannabis; specifically, *toke* refers to the action of aggressively and repeatedly combusting a bowl in a pipe or a bong; often combined with the word *up*, as in *toke up*, presumably to allude to the forthcoming state of being; —*toker* *n.* one who smokes or tokes cannabis; Steve Miller; *see The Joker*

tool box- *n. see tackle box*

topicals (topical)- *n.pl.* the term used to describe the collective group of cannabis products designed to be applied topically to the skin instead of being ingested; *topicals* include lotions, balms, salves, creams, soaps, lubes, and scrubs

topper- *n.* that which is added to the top of a bowl of cannabis flowers in order to increase potency, flavor, or smoke quality; a *topper* can be a dab, some kief or hash, or other cannabis flowers of superior quality to the bowl filler below; *see bowl filler*

top shelf- *n.* the best-of-the-best cannabis flowers available at a specific dispensary; —*top-shelf adj.* having the characteristics of the top shelf; *top shelf* comes from a bar term representing the location of the best bottles of booze; named *connoisseur shelf* by those dispensaries understanding the sin that is alcohol or simply want to sound pretentious; just because a place labels something *top shelf* or connoisseur shelf, does not mean that it actually is; make sure that you educate yourself, so that you aren't fooled into believing the bullshit hype; *for differentiation see compassion shelf, bottom shelf, midgrade*

topsoil- *n.* the uppermost layer of soil in a garden that is often difficult to cultivate without being heavily amended

torch- *n.* the type of lighter needed by dabbers to heat their nails, often a small blowtorch or culinary *torch;* also, a colloquial term for a joint; —*v.* to dab; to ignite a joint or bowl; —*torch it v.* to combust cannabis; —*torched adj.* stoned

total cannabinoid profile- *n.* the percentage of each cannabinoid viewed collectively for a particular cannabis sample; a *total cannabinoid profile* of a strain will include levels of THC, CBD, CBN, THCv, CBC, and CBG; *i.e. In this day and age, any cannabis flower sample that does not have a total cannabinoid profile in the twenty to forty percent range is considered lower potency cannabis.*

tote- *n.* a large volume of soil or amendment sold for cannabis cultivation, usually approximately one cubic yard or more

trace minerals- *n.pl.* the group of approximately seventy minerals and elements not commonly found in prepared fertilizers, but are necessary for cannabis growth; natural, organic soil is rich in *trace minerals* and requires no application of them without a documented deficiency; *trace minerals* can compound in soil and remain in plant tissues, leading to potentially toxic, poisonous or lethal levels of heavy metals; use of these should be avoided at all costs unless there is a verified deficiency that needs a correction; *see heavy metal toxicity*

Trainwreck- *n.* a sativa dominant heirloom cannabis strain supposedly naturalized to Northern California that grows very vinelike; one of the few sativas to adapt to Northern Cali's unique, more indica-suited climate; although *Trainwreck* is purportedly named after how the plant was discovered, the moniker is rather apt in effect as well

traveler- *n.* a small dab rig used for travel; *for differentiation, see kit*

195

tree- *n.* a juvenile colloquialism for cannabis based on the perceived shape of mature cannabis flowers; *i.e. I heard the poser point to me and announce to the party: 'He be puffin' on fyah tree, yaknowaddimean dawg!?!' Not cool... on so many different levels.*

tree hugger- *n.* one who smokes fyah tree

Triangle Kush- *n.* an indica dominant cannabis hybrid (or phenotype) of *OG Kush* from Florida in the 1990s; she gets her name from the major cannabis producing areas of Florida at the time: Jacksonville, Miami, and Tampa; some people believe *Triangle Kush* to be the mother of all *OGs*, but the truth about the strain is lost somewhere in Bermuda

trichomes- *n.pl.* the fine outgrowths or hairs on plants; there are two main types of *trichomes* in cannabis: *glandular* and *cystolithic*; glandular *trichomes* are the capitulate hairs on cannabis that produce and release aromatic resins full of cannabinoids and terpenes; glandular *trichomes* give cannabis its characteristic crystalline appearance and characteristic stickiness; cystolithic *trichomes* serve to protect the glandular *trichomes* and produce no resin

trichs (trikes)- *abbrv. see trichomes*

trim- *v.* to cut or remove the large fan and other leaves from harvested cannabis prior to manicuring; *for differentiation, see manicure —n.* the remnants leftover from the manicuring or trimming process; *see sugar leaf*

Trinity- *n.* an unknown sativa dominant heirloom cannabis strain bred by Jeremy P. in Kansas; *Trinity* was dispersed to growers in Oregon who have since spread the strain throughout the West, especially The Emerald Triangle in California; numerous strains out of Northern California must claim *Trinity* in their ancestry, nearly to the point of a bit of redundancy in strain similarity from the region in the last ten years (like that which has occurred with

Granddaddy Purple and *Mendo Purps*... can y'all breed with some new shit, please?)

Trinity County- *n.* the less popular location of the some of world's greatest outdoor cannabis cultivation; *Trinity County* is partially responsible for supplying the entire US with the majority of its cannabis; *for differentiation, see Emerald Triangle, Humboldt County, Mendocino County*

tri-nodality- *n.* a cannabis trait where there are three branch or bud sites at every node, instead of the typical two for indica dominant strains, or one for some sativa dominant strains; offspring with *tri-nodality* produce thirty-three percent more flowers per branch due to the increase in bud sites; *tri-nodality* is a very rare recessive trait that appears to be triggered by a viral stimuli and most growers go their whole lives without ever seeing it; *i.e. Several Love Genetics strains are bred with parents who had tri-nodality, and select phenotypes will represent with this trait.*

truncheon- *n.* a specific type of cannabis nutrient solution wand meter that gets its name from the fact that it is shaped like the baton used by peaceful keepers of the law to bludgeon to death dirty pothead hippies, blacks and Mexicans

trykes- *n.pl. see trichomes*

t-shirt press- *n.* the eponymous item that is used by larger scale extract artists to make rosin; *see rosin, hair straightener*

tube- *n.* colloquial for a dab rig, and, occasionally, a bong

tumbler- *n.* a device used to separate the glandular trichomes from the vegetative cannabis material by tossing the flowers in a screened cylinder in order to make kief

turning Japanese- *phr. derogatory see squinty-eyed*

tweed- *n. see weed;* also, that which could be easily replaced with hemp fibers

twelve-twelve (12-12, 12/12)- *n.* the photoperiod cycle required to force cannabis to flower in an artificial environment equal to twelve hours of light and twelve hours of dark

twenty- *n.* a quantity of cannabis worth twenty dollars; *$20* is the amount of money charged for a gram of top-shelf retail cannabis that actually costs less than fractions of a cent to produce on a commercial scale by a consummate cannabis cultivator

twig- *n.* low quality or stemmy cannabis; *i.e. I canna never cruz to dat place ova by da college cuza de only carry da twig n de blasted buds.*

twist one up (twist one, twist one off)- *v.* to roll a joint; the term comes from the traditional act of twisting a paper to hold it together instead of using a glue; now, the term simply refers to rolling a joint, or the twisting off of the end of a newly rolled joint like one might bite off the end of a cigar; *i.e. Have y'all ever seen Willie twist one up? Man, that guy's lightning!*

twisted (twisty)- *adj.* having the quality or characteristic of being high, especially off a joint; *i.e. Let go score a baggie of some dank shit and get fuckin' twisted!*

twisters- *n.pl.* joints

twomp- *n.* a ghetto colloquial term for an amount of cannabis equal to twenty dollars worth; *i.e. Beep me on my pager if you wiggaz eva need a twomp.*

two thousand dollars ($2000)- *n.* typically, the minimum amount of money paid by a dispensary for one pound of cannabis flowers; the going rate for one pound of outdoor cannabis; if one is a provider earning less than *$2000* per pound, then he needs to do one of two things: learn to grow, or peddle his wares elsewhere; in general, cannabis wholesales for $1300 to $5000 per pound, depending on quality, location and market saturation, and available resources or connections; *i.e. Even though I don't sell flowers, I've been offered $2700 for my outdoor and $5000 for my indoor, so why would I ever settle for the going rate of $2000?*

vacuum oven- *n. see purging oven*

Valhalla- *n.* a sativa dominant cannabis strain bred by Love Genetics that is the polyhybrid *ACDC x Purple Dragon Kush x Jack Herer x White Siberian*; one of the first high CBD, high THC strains with a 1:1 ratio and a total cannabinoid profile over twenty percent; *Valhalla* is the mother to the famous *Valkyrie (Valhalla x Jack Phoenix #2)*

vape (vaporize)- *v.* to heat cannabis flowers to the point of evaporating the active cannabinoids without combusting the vegetal material; *vaping* is the healthiest way to inhale cannabis, but less pleasurable to purists; anyone truly wanting to be a healthy medical cannabis patient should only use pure, clean, tested juices, caps or extracts, or, at the very most, *vape* pure, clean, organic meds and solvent-less concentrates

vape pen- *n.* a portable personal vaporizer so named for its shape and relative size to a large writing pen; due to the potential of explosion, use of these is not recommended

vaporizer- *n.* a specific type of cannabis implement that heats ground flower parts to a set temperature, instead of combusting them, in order to release the terpenes and activated cannabinoids with the evaporating water vapor

variety- *n. see strain*

Vedas, the- *n.* ancient (2000-1400 BC) and sanctified Hindi religious texts that clearly classify cannabis as a sacred plant given to humans to help us lose fear and attain joy; according to *the Vedas*, cannabis is a liberator and an ultimate source of joy with a guardian angel living within her leaves; God has been telling us about cannabis for a long ass time, you know

vega- *n.* the cigar equivalent of a secret agent; a *vega* is ostensibly a blunt that is stuffed rather than rolled; *vega* is not to be confused with *verga*, which is also something on which some people suck

veg room- *n.* in indoor cannabis cultivation, this is the room specifically for cannabis plants that are in their vegetative state of growth; a *veg room* is typically set for eighteen hours of light and six hours of dark, though some ambitious and wealthy growers keep the light on for twenty-four hours to achieve the same or worse effect

veganic (veganic cannabis)- *n.* cannabis that has been grown organically and without the use of any animal products; supposedly makes the best tasting, most nutritious and cannabinoid packed medicine; —*adj.* having the characteristic of *veganic cannabis*

veggies- *n.pl.* a colloquialism for cannabis, presumably based on the fact that it is nutritious and healthy for one's body like vegetables; *i.e. Call your homeboy, Herb, and get some veggies for us, yo… I'm starvin' for that shit!*

vendor- *n.* a cannabis provider who must pay taxes; *for differentiation, see provider*

verification- *n.* a medical cannabis prescription available from a legal, board-certified doctor of medicine; imagine that, your doctor says cannabis is safe to use for an abundance of ailments… approximately 700, to be more precise

vermiculite- *n.* an amendment used in cannabis cultivation that is a hydrothermal alteration of certain minerals; *vermiculite* helps aerate the soil without reducing moisture retention

vermiganics (vermiculture)- *n.* a type of cannabis cultivation that uses a soil or soilless mix built upon a foundation of worm castings

veterans- *n.pl.* one of the largest, loudest and most worthy medical cannabis advocacy populations in the US and the world

vertical gardening- *n.* a specific type of indoor cannabis cultivation that stacks multiple layers of cannabis plants under LED or fluorescent lights on tall, industrial shelves; the square footage of a grow room doubles for every shelf employed in a *vertical gardening* set up

violetglass- *n.* a specific type of ultraviolet-protected glass that is used to make jars and bottles for long-term cannabis storage

Vireo Health of New York- *n.* the innovative New York medical cannabis provider that is the first in the nation to have its products certified Kosher; amen, sisters and brothers, and shalom!

Vitamin D- *n.* a dab or other concentrate used for dabbing; *Vitamin D* is not a vitamin, and should not be mistaken for the healthy dose of dick taken as a morning supplement in a happy union

Volcano- *n.* a specific type of home vaporizer that heats the cannabis such that the vapors are off-gassed into a plastic bag for the user to empty as he sees fit; yes, when it is outlined simply, it does seem like an asinine concept: hey, I've got a great idea… let's take the safest way to inhale cannabis vapor and make it potentially toxic by leaving it in a fucking plastic bag; *i.e. I overheard someone sincerely ask if the plastic bag ban was going to affect his potential to purchase any necessary Volcano replacement bags.;* also, a *volcano* is an illuminated lampshade that erupts cannabis smoke from a hit or due to air flow in a hotboxed room

voluntary patient registry- *n.* in Washington State, and potentially in California and other areas, this is the *elective* list medical patients must add their name to in order to access the right to all of their medicine; the federal government has admittedly used these lists for the purposes of prosecuting federal drug violations; a *voluntary patient registry* is like having severely ill US citizens sew yellow stars onto our clothes and get numbered tattoos on our forearms... what's next?... putting us in camps and lining us up for the incinerator?

wacky tobacky (wocci tobacci)- *n.* a ridiculous colloquialism for cannabis used to describe the fallaciously perceived outcome of intoxication on the cannabis user: pioneer psychosis

wacky weed- *n. see weed, wacky tobacky*

wake 'n' bake (wake and bake)- *v.* the term given to awaking to a fresh bowl of pot rather than a steamy pot of coffee; to wake up from sleep in the morning (afternoon) and immediately smoke or vape cannabis; *i.e. When I was much younger, I used to love a good wake 'n' bake. Now, I prefer to wake up a little bit...like two or three minutes before I medicate.*

WAMM- *acronym* the Wo/Men's Alliance for Medical Marijuana; effectively the only federally *legal* medical cannabis provider in the nation, founded by Valerie and Mike Corral in Santa Cruz, California; *WAMM* is now operated by Val and its collective members, and is on the cutting edge of experiential medical research and unsanctioned human trials on the efficacy of medical cannabis for the treatment of serious or terminal illnesses such as cancer, Parkinson's, epilepsy, and bigotry; to date, *WAMM* has effectively assisted patients in *curing* cancer and recovering from other life debilitating illnesses; *see Rice, Ben and Krohn, Christopher*

wand- *n. see dab tool;* also, a *wand* is a type of spray nozzle attachment and a type of testing meter used in cannabis cultivation

War on Drugs, The- *n.* the proper name for the improper and violently excessive assault on world citizens who choose to consume cannabis, or illegal drugs; in fact, *The War on Drugs* is actually a *war on people (of color especially);* the disproportionately vast majority of victims in this brutal and unforgiving, reprehensible jihad against a country's own citizenry are black or of ethnic or foreign decent; at some point, we the people will have had enough of *The War on Drugs*, and, if the federal government continues to persist, may actually begin to fight back in a civil war for drugs; leave cannabis users be, and start fucking fighting the real crimes like rape, abuse, and murder, gov

wash- *v.* to quickly saturate cannabis plant material with an often dangerous or poisonous solvent in order to extract the resins; *see blast*

washing machine- *n. see bubble machine*

water cure- *v.* to repeatedly soak freshly cut cannabis flowers in a zero ppm distilled or filtered water in order to leach out all remaining salts in the cannabis material prior to drying and traditionally curing them; the end result of a *water cure* is often a flower that tests out at a higher potency due to the lack of moisture content and residual biochemicals, but is papery or artificial feeling; a great way to risk losing all of your harvest to mold or other contaminants; —*water-cured adj.* having the quality or characteristic of cannabis that has undergone a water cure

water pipe (waterpipe)- *n. see bong*

wax- *n.* a type of solvent-extracted cannabis concentrate that gets its name from the waxlike consistency that allows the dabber to roll tiny balls of it up and place on the nail head; poetic, like this dictionary

weed- *n.* a common colloquialism for cannabis, possibly based on the fact that it grows feral like weeds in areas with landraces or naturalized cannabis strains

Weed Belt- *n.* a derogatory euphemism for the Green Belt; *see Green Belt*

weedery- *n.* a derogatory euphemism for a cannabisery; *see cannabisery*

Weedmaps- *n.* an online resource for cannabis users to locate cannabis dispensaries, doctors, or coffee shops in legal states and countries; *for differentiation, see Leafly*

weed people- *n.pl. see drama*

Weeds- *n.* a Showtime television series airing from 2005 to 2012 that was loosely based on the hyperbolic *real* life of a housewife pot dealer

Weed Wars- *n.* a cancelled Discovery Channel documentary series on cannabis that aired in 2011

weight loss- *n.* one of the wonderful side effects of smoking or consuming high THCv (and occasionally high THC) cannabis and may be the means by which cannabis is finally legalized; *i.e. If all the chunky women of the world realized that cannabis can safely help them achieve the weight loss they want, then no man or partner would have sex ever again until cannabis was as legal as a tomato worldwide.*

Werc Shop, The- *n.* a famous cannabis testing lab that is known for collaborating with the University of Southern California to write a peer review study on cannabis concentrates: *Understanding dabs: contamination concerns of cannabis concentrates and cannabinoid transfer during the act of dabbing* by Jeffrey C. Raber, Sytze Elzinga and Charles Kaplan

wetting agent- *n. see surfactant*

whip- *v.* to manually beat fresh cannabis concentrate in order to bring more of the residual solvents to the surface and assist in purging by exposing it to air; —*n.* the apparatus used with a home vaporizer that consists of a mouthpiece on one end of a tube or shaft and an oven on the other; —*v.* what cannabis advocates are going to do to staunch prohibitionists at the voting booths… if they can just manage to remember to care enough to GET OFF OF THE COUCH AND VOTE

whiteflies (white flies)- *n.pl.* small flying insects in the Aleyrodidea family that feed by sucking on the undersides of leaves; *whiteflies* love to feed on certain strains of cannabis and must be monitored and controlled for well when cultivating outdoors

White Russian- *n.* a sativa dominant cannabis strain bred by Serious Seeds that is *AK-47 x White Widow;* in this case as in all, the cannabis derivative far outweighs the alcoholic drink; a great thing about *White Russian* is that certain phenotypes smell and taste like cream soda

White Widow- *n.* an indica dominant cannabis strain bred by Green House Seed Co. that is *Brazilian x South Indian;* winner of the 1995 *High Times* Cannabis Cup; there is a great deal of drama and misinformation available on the real history of who actually bred this strain; the most aggressively vocal and outspoken breeder to claim *White Widow* is Shantibaba aka "Shantiblahblah"; in an eloquent and scathing open letter from Arjan of Green House Seed Co., Shantibaba's claims are refuted, and he is relegated to being only "the water boy" at the time that Arjan and the other legitimate heads of Green House actually bred the legendary strain; decide for yourself, because, like Nick Carraway, I try not to color things with judgment

whole plant- *n.* the most medically beneficial part of the cannabis plant; in reality, *whole plant* refers specifically to the aerial parts of the fully flowered sensimilla cannabis plant; *see entourage effect; —whole-plant adj.* having the characteristics of *whole-plant* cannabis or cannabis medicine; *whole-plant* medicine is considered to be the most effective due to the over three hundred potentially medically beneficial compounds found in the Cannabis genus

winterization- *n.* the process of making an absolute using alcohol and freezing temperatures; *see absolute, dewax*

wizard (Wizard of Oz)- *n.* a colloquial term for an ounce of cannabis; *i.e. Be suspicious if your preteen says he's off to see* *the wizard, the wonderful Wizard of Oz, and he is not a Broadway enthusiast… he's likely a different kind of flamer, wearing a different kind of blazer.*

Women Grow- *n.* an organization founded by women that was "created to connect, educate, inspire and empower the next generation of cannabis industry leaders by creating programs, community and events for aspiring and current business executives; *Women Grow* is a for-profit entity that serves as a catalyst for women to influence and succeed in the cannabis industry as the end of cannabis prohibition occurs on a national scale"; I quote them because women are always accusing me of twisting their words around, even when I remember verbatim

wood ash- *n.* an amendment used in organic cannabis cultivation that is high in potash; *see potash*

Woodstock- *n.* the infamous 1969 concert held near Woodstock, New York that everyone's cool hippie mom, dad, and uncle went to, but was actually only attended by roughly four hundred thousand people; to some, *Woodstock* was a revelation, but to most it was the demarcation of the end of an era: thus, the hippies had gone too far for the government to ignore anymore, and they were too weak not to become assimilated (just ask your cool hippie banker mom, dope druggist dad, and unctuous CEO uncle)

worm castings- *n.pl.* worm shit; *worm castings* are used heavily in organic cannabis cultivation as a soil conditioner, biological activator, and mild fertilizer; *see vermiganics*

wrecked- *adj.* so stoned that one has crashed into the couch

yardie- *n.* a British colloquialism used to describe a Jamaican gang; actually, it probably just meant a buncha da kid di bi smokin' di yarndie

yarndie- *n.* a Jamaican colloquial term for cannabis

yellow submarine- *n.* colloquial for a joint, based on the Beatles' eponymous song

your nose knows, you know- phr. the popular or common wisdom suggesting that smelling a strain of cannabis and finding it pleasing or appetizing is the best way to determine if it's the right strain for one's personal or medical need; *your nose knows, you know* is along the same lines as craving a food that is rich in a vitamin in which one may be deficient

yucca- *n.* a genus of shrubs that produce natural surfactants and is often used in cannabis nutrients, mediums, and fertilizers

zeppelin- *n.* a specific type of one-hitter similar to a bat; *see one-hitter, bat*

zig- *n.* a joint; *see Zig Zag*

Zig Zag- *n.* a French rolling paper that was often used in the recent past to roll cannabis; *Zig Zags* are no longer in vogue for cannabis smokers due to the fact that the papers are made from flax, not hemp, and are usually bleached

Zimbabwe weed- *n.* this shit turns you into a deer; *see Grandma's Boy*

zoot- *n.* a spliff or joint, especially one smoked by a rioter in the 1940s or one who wears the suit of said agitator

zooted- *adj.* another, hopefully the last, asinine colloquialism for being extremely high, drunk, or both; *i.e. I hope to soon live in an area where people do not use the word zooted... not because they are snobby pretentious douchebags, but because they would never crossfade for the sake of their health.*

Z.Z.Z. (Zip. Zero. Zilch.)- *n.* the number of deaths directly caused by or solely attributed to cannabis use; a rather amazing statistic; *i.e. The LD 50 (lethal dose) of THC is around 42-60 mg of PURE THC per kilogram of body weight consumed all at one time without the presence of CBD, which is virtually a physical impossibility. The biggest stoner in the world could never intentionally smoke that much at one time, and it would be quite difficult to find and consume that much pure THC orally. To put it in perspective, the lethal dose of alcohol is 0.4% BAC and is responsible for killing hundreds of thousands of people worldwide every year. A person can easily drink enough, especially in a party situation, to achieve a lethal dose without ever being aware of it. Just ask the parents of all the teenagers who never woke up after a night of drinking. Furthermore, any alcohol can be a lethal dose for any drinker or bystander when combined with the sadly yet oft-used mixer, the vehicle.; also, Z.Z.Z. represents the number of excuses you, me, the government* and the world's population have to not legalize cannabis, especially for medical use; *i.e. Now that you know that there are Zip. Zero. Zilch. reasons to vilify cannabis, why not get lit as fuck with me?*

ABOUT THE AUTHOR

Jason Porter Collinsworth is a well-known breeder, author, and musician in the budding cannabis industry. He has been featured in the *East Bay Express*, *The Cannifornian*, the *Sacramento News and Review*, *Good Times Santa Cruz*, *The Stockton Record*, the *San Diego Jewish Journal*, and *News21*.

Collinsworth began working with cannabis in 1996 while attending UC Santa Cruz but only seriously focused his efforts in 2011. After contracting a rare disorder that nearly took his life, Collinsworth had to medically retire from teaching high school English, producing the biannual drama performances, and coaching the league-winning girls soccer team.

He then founded Love Genetics and initiated innovative, specialized breeding programs designed specifically to combine high CBD and high THC cannabis genetics. Collinsworth's genetics are known worldwide and are featured on the largest and most comprehensive genetics database, *seedfinder.eu*.

Collinsworth used his experience and research in the field of cannabis to write *The Unrevealed Series*, a trilogy about a cannabis breeder turned superhero. He also released a poetry anthology entitled *Tearing Apart a Whisper*, a cannabis dictionary called *The Doobieous Dictionary: The A-Z Guide to All Things Cannabis,* and the cannabis party games guide, *High Jinx: Cannabis Party Games & Activities,* along with his debut cookbook, *Women Love a Man Who Can Cook.*

Under the stage name of The Gateway Affect, Collinsworth and his wife, Summer Dazed, recently dropped their first hip-hop/pop album, *Cali Grrrl,* and are currently working on their second project.

Collinsworth continues to produce music and write while living in Central California with his wife, two kids, and four cats.

Connect with Jason online

http://www.lovegenetics.org
https://summerdazed420.com

Twitter:
@GatewayAffect
@JP_Collinsworth
@UnrevealedNovel

YouTube:
http://www.youtube.com/c/JasonPorterCollinsworth

Also Available from Jason Porter Collinsworth (The Gateway Affect)

Cali Grrrl-
A fun California hip-hop album by *Summer Dazed & The Gateway Affect* featuring the tracks:

1 We're High Society
2 Slippery Slide
3 Cali Grrrl
4 Firefly
5 Bong Bounce
6 Island Blues
7 Exes & Hos
8 Ghostin'
9 Livin' in Paradise
10 Silverwhite
11 Never Comin' Down
12 Stand with Me (Freestyle)
13 More Than a Girl
https://summerdazed420.com

The Unrevealed Series: Book #1

Haze Kalu is determined to correct the sins of his mysterious past. He breeds cannabis strains designed to heal the terminally ill, especially Estella, the five-year-old niece of his best friend. He wants nothing more than to grow his cannabis and to save people's lives. But savagery once again seeks Haze out, and he violently discovers his hidden powers. As Haze struggles to make sense of his supernatural abilities, he meets Jade, a luscious psychic with an acid tongue and a lethal ass who absorbs the energy of others. Unsure of Jade's intentions, Haze becomes allies with her while vicious forces begin hunting them. The two endeavor to find the evil trying to destroy Haze before it's too late and Estella dies.

THE CONVERGENCE

JASON PORTER COLLINSWORTH
LARA MARIE COLLINSWORTH

The Unrevealed Series: Book #2

Following a destructive battle, Haze Kalu and Jade Renata seek out answers to their mysterious origins and destiny. Now that Haze's superhero abilities have graduated to their fullest extent, he and Jade join forces with their friends to continue fighting demons and search for the ultimate evil, The Red Butterfly. With the help of Haze's best friend, Rasul Williams, Jade and Haze learn their true nature and the celestial provenance of their powers. When he finds out that his ultimate nemesis is the missing piece of the puzzle, Haze must cast his past aside and embrace the truth in order to save humanity.

COMING SOON

The Unrevealed Series: Book #3

Will Jade survive?
Who is the Red Butterfly?
What happens in Death Valley?
How will it end?

Light up your next party!

A collection of over 50 cannabis games and activities for you and your friends to play at your next pot party. With various levels of expertise from Cannanewbie to Bong Lord, there is something for everyone. Whether you are looking for a cannabis twist on an old favorite like *Bong Pong* or something completely wild and new like *Drop a Dime Bag* or *Pineapple Expression*, *High Jinks* is fun for all. Full of card games, dice games, and adult play, this book is sure to burn your bowl.

High and Go Seek   Crazy Eighths   Blunty Questions   Sparko Polo
Pin the Pipe on the Hippie   Bong Lords and Posers   Sativa
Scavenger Hunt   500 Pounds   and more…

Recipes That Impress

Delicious, easily-made-from-scratch original recipes that will make you a hit with any crowd… especially the ladies. After all, women love a man who can cook!